THE
ERNST & YOUNG
BUSINESS PLAN
GUIDE

Second Edition

Also from Ernst & Young

The Ernst & Young Guide to Total Cost Management
The Complete Guide to Special Event Management
The Ernst & Young Guide to Raising Capital
The Ernst & Young Guide to Expanding in the Global Market
*Understanding and Using Financial Data: An Ernst & Young Guide
   for Attorneys*

Forthcoming from Ernst & Young

The Ernst & Young Guide to Mergers & Acquisitions, Second Edition
The Ernst & Young World Markets Resource Guide 1993–1994
The Ernst & Young Guide to Managing Information Strategically
   (An Ernst & Young Information Technology book)
The Ernst & Young Guide to Development Effectiveness (An Ernst
   & Young Information Technology book)

The Ernst & Young Business Plan Guide

Second Edition

Eric S. Siegel
Brian R. Ford
Jay M. Bornstein

John Wiley & Sons, Inc.
New York • Chichester • Brisbane • Toronto • Singapore

This text is printed on acid-free paper.

This book formerly appeared as *The Arthur Young Business Plan Guide*
Copyright © 1987 by Arthur Young.

Copyright © 1993 by Ernst & Young
Published by John Wiley & Sons, Inc.

Library of Congress Cataloging in Publication Data:

Siegel, Eric S.
    The Ernst & Young business plan guide (originally
    published as The Arthur Young business plan guide).
    Bibliography: p.
    Includes index.
    1. New business enterprises.   I.
II. Ford, Brian R.   III. Title.
HD62.5.S556   1987   658.4'012   86-32622
    ISBN 0-471-57825-8
    ISBN 0-471-57826-6 (pbk.)

Printed in the United States of America

10 9 8 7 6 5 4 3 2 1

The authors wish to thank the following people for their invaluable counsel and assistance on this book:

Jon Zonderman
Robin M. Siegel
Loren Schultz

PREFACE

This book has been prepared for entrepreneurs who are in the planning stages of starting, expanding, or acquiring a business. It provides a step-by-step procedure for preparing a business plan. The instruction goes beyond simply discussing what is required in such a proposal. It explains why certain information is required, how it may be best presented, and the sensitivities of both the preparer and reviewer.

Many entrepreneurs underestimate the importance of writing a business plan. They underestimate how much having a good business plan can help a new business to raise money to start or expand, plan for the future, and keep tabs on how it is currently progressing. In this book, we will not only stress these important aspects of business plans, but help the entrepreneur think through and prepare a business plan that will serve all three purposes.

Launching a business venture is a serious undertaking. While statistics on the failure rate of new businesses vary, all suggest a high incidence, particularly in the first few years. Acquisitions of existing businesses or product lines and expansions of present operations enjoy a significantly higher success rate, due to the lesser degree of uncertainty. However, even in these circumstances, issues are complex and stakes are high.

In light of this, entrepreneurs must act in whatever manner will improve these odds. In almost every instance, this suggests the meticulous creation and following of a business plan. The exercise of writing a business plan will force the entrepreneur to examine each element of his or her prospective venture closely. It is expected that many cracks and flaws will be identified and addressed through this process.

Where such problems cannot be addressed and where their ramifications are significant, the fact that they have been identified affords the entrepreneur an opportunity to abandon the venture before resources have been committed.

In the first three chapters of this book, some of the basics of business plans are laid out. Chapter 1 asks: What is a business plan? A business plan has more purposes than the one most people think of first—that of raising money.

Many entrepreneurs misunderstand who reads a business plan and what those readers are looking for. In Chapter 2, we discuss both lenders and investors, and how they evaluate a business plan.

Chapter 3 deals with the legal form a business may take. What form a business takes is an important determinant of the amount of money that can be raised for the business and from whom, the form of the infusion, the impact the federal tax code will have on the business, and the potential financial rewards for investors.

The vast majority of this book, beginning with Chapter 4, consists of a piece-by-piece dissection of a model business plan. In each of these chapters, a portion of the business plan is examined. Suggestions are made on how entrepreneurs should structure and present parts of the plan. Questions and issues to which an entrepreneur must be sensitive when preparing the plan are examined. Finally, questions that will be asked by an individual who reviews the plan are raised.

In each of the chapters that deal with a specific part of the business plan, we will provide a general narrative dealing with how to think through and prepare this portion of the plan. A portion of a model business plan will next be presented. The business plan we use is for Good Foods, Inc. (GFI), an all-natural baby and children's food company. The plan is hypothetical and has been prepared by the authors as an example for illustrative purposes.

After each section of the GFI business plan is presented, the authors will comment on it, pointing out its strong and weak points. The likely reactions of reviewers are also presented.

The three sections of each chapter are presented in three different typefaces for ease of reading. We believe this book will be valuable in the development of a professional and effective business plan.

ERIC S. SIEGEL
BRIAN R. FORD
JAY M. BORNSTEIN

Paoli, Pennsylvania
Philadelphia, Pennsylvania
January 1993

≡ ABOUT THE AUTHORS ≡

Eric Siegel has consulted with entrepreneurs, growth companies, turnaround companies, and acquisition candidates since 1980. In 1983, he formed Siegel Management Company, where he has prepared and reviewed numerous business plans, arranged financings and participated in the management of client companies. He is also an owner and developer of the Paoli Technology Enterprise Center, a business incubator located in suburban Philadelphia, and a lecturer in entrepreneurial management at the Wharton School.

Brian Ford, an audit partner in the Philadelphia office of Ernst & Young, has many years of experience specializing in services to entrepreneurial businesses. He has been instrumental in the early development of the Entrepreneurial Services Group practice in Philadelphia, a full-service organization specifically designed to provide services to growing businesses. He has worked with entrepreneurs from their "idea" stage to beyond their initial public offering.

Jay Bornstein, a tax partner in the Philadelphia office of Ernst & Young, has served as a tax advisor to entrepreneurial businesses and their owners for over twenty years. His clients include start-up businesses which eventually grew to become publicly traded companies to management buy-outs of business units of some of the country's largest companies.

CONTENTS

1

THE BUSINESS PLAN

WHAT IS A BUSINESS PLAN AND WHY WRITE ONE?

Entrepreneurs are most often doers rather than proposal writers. They would rather be on the battlefield—the cutting edge of business—than behind the lines planning their assault. In addition, many entrepreneurs have difficulty articulating the business concepts that have often become second nature to them.

Consequently, one of the most difficult chores they face is the preparation and actual writing of a business plan. Whatever difficulty the preparation of a business plan may present, a plan is an absolute necessity for any business.

A business plan serves three functions. First, and foremost, it is a *plan* that can be used to develop ideas about how the business should be conducted. It is a chance to refine strategies and "make mistakes on paper" rather than in the real world, by examining the company from all perspectives, such as marketing, finance, and operations. Second, a business plan is a retrospective tool, against which a businessperson can assess a company's actual performance over time. For example, the financial part of a business plan can be used as the basis for an operating budget, and can be monitored carefully to see how closely the business is sticking to that budget. In this regard, the plan can and should be used as the basis for a new plan. After some time has elapsed, and thereafter on a periodic basis, the business plan should be examined to see where and even why the company strayed, whether that straying was helpful or harmful, and how the business should operate in the future.

The third reason for writing a business plan is the one most people think of first, that is, to raise money. Most lenders or investors will not put money into a business without seeing a business plan. There are stories of wild-eyed entrepreneurs and venture capitalists with pens at the ready who meet, scribble some projections on a wet cocktail napkin, shake hands, and become "partners" in a hot technology business, but those are myths.

But even during the earlier years of the modern venture capital boom, the mid- and late-1970s, when there may have been less formality and more dynamism in the venture capital world, there was always an orderly process for securing venture capital. A large part of that process is the preparation and examination of a business plan.

If an entrepreneur presents an idea to a commercial lender or a potential investor without a business plan in hand, that money source will ask the entrepreneur to draft one and come back later. Or worse, the potential source of money may not take the entrepreneur seriously, and may not ask the entrepreneur back at all. Assuming that he or she invites the entrepreneur back, the entrepreneur may wish to seek professional assistance in writing the plan, perhaps from a consultant or an accountant. The bottom line, however, is that a formal, written plan must be prepared if the venture and the funding request is to be taken seriously.

A business plan is a document designed to map out the course of a company over a specific period of time. Many companies write annual business plans, which focus intently on the coming 12 months and give more general attention about the following one to four years. Few business plans project beyond five years.

Because the business plan is a hybrid document—part pragmatic projection and part sales tool—it must walk a fine line in content and tone of presentation. The information must be accurate, yet must convey a sense of optimism and excitement. Although risks must be acknowledged, they should not be dwelled on.

The tone should be businesslike. If there is too much schmaltz, people won't take the plan seriously. But the people who read business plans are real people. They will respond to a positive, interesting presentation, and will be turned off by one that is vague, long-winded, or not well thought out and organized. They may also read so many business plans in a week that their eyes glaze over. Therefore a business plan that makes especially good use of graphics, or that paints a picture of the company in a provocative way, has a better chance of being looked at closely than one that is monotonous and gray. Even minor errors in spelling and grammar can suggest substantial negatives regarding the entrepreneur and therefore the entire enterprise. Have someone skilled in this area review the plan to eliminate these minor annoyances that may have a major impact on the reader.

PLANNING NEEDS TO BE DYNAMIC

Even when typewriters were still in vogue a friend said that Rule 1 for preparing a business plan is, "Do it on a word processor." Another colleague always packages business plans in a three-ring binder. The message is clear. Business plans are ephemeral, they are constantly subject to change and adjustment. The preparation of a business plan must be seen as an iterative process, as both the assumptions and the projections those assumptions engender must be constantly refined. And the preparation of a business plan never really stops.

It usually takes months to obtain financing. While a financing can be closed in as little as three months, this is the speed of light in the business world, and six or more months is often more realistic. Some potential sources of funding may want to see updates of the plan, fresh thoughts, or updated financial figures if the company is already doing business.

While a company may formally rewrite a business plan every year, it may want to monitor and update the plan more frequently, perhaps quarterly or even monthly.

LOOKING FORWARD—THE BUSINESS PLAN AS A PLANNING DOCUMENT

Many people who think "business plan" think "start-up company." Yet this is not necessarily accurate. Ongoing companies should and often do create business plans.

Federal Express, one of the granddaddies of the modern venture capital culture and still one of the largest venture capital investments ever—over $70 million—still prepares an annual business plan.

For an ongoing business, the business plan serves a number of functions. It is a way of getting consensus and consistency throughout the company. While business plans of rank start-ups are often written by one or two people, in an ongoing company—especially one that is larger—a number of people will have a hand in writing the business plan.

By the time the business plan has run through a number of revisions and is produced in final form, nearly everyone involved will have been involved in preparing the plan's vision for the company.

A frequent complaint from those running existing small businesses is that, because of the day-to-day management pressures involved in a small company, there is precious little time for planning. This is, of course, unfortunate, since a continuing effort at business planning is probably more important to the survival of a small company than to a large company.

The business plan is, in many ways, a company's first crack at strategic planning. And, contrary to what many people think, strategic planning not only can be done in the context of a small company, but is vital, as a small company often does not have the resources that would allow it to recover from mistakes.

The business plan is also an implementation tool. It can be used to test theories of how the company should be run and to calculate possible outcomes. Then the plan can be checked as those ideas are implemented to see if the projections were accurate. This step provides an early-warning system and allows for prompt action to correct problems.

Ongoing companies or those acquiring existing businesses have an advantage over new companies when developing a business plan. The numbers they use to make projections will have some basis in fact and experience. And the strategies they outline for the business's future will also be rooted in their past strategies, incorporating what the company gained from its successes and learned from its mistakes.

Many of the questions one needs to ask to prepare a business plan must be successfully answered, or at least put in the "can't be answered at this time but must be monitored" folder, if a company is going to survive.

Sometimes a key question is overlooked. For instance, a promising small specialty chemical company forgot to ask itself about the impact of federal environmental regulations before starting up its business. The company went into production in 1983, anticipating the first sales in 1984. It hired personnel, opened an office, and began marketing. With the meter running—the company was incurring significant overhead—the company finally discovered that it would need a Federal Environmental Protection Agency (EPA) review of its products before it could actively market them. The company nearly bled itself dry maintaining its facilities and personnel while its product was tied up in review. This particular company made it, but others aren't so lucky.

Another company's business plan was good enough to acquire financing. The company was going to provide technical studio facilities for the production of audio and video products.

On the level of a business concept, the plan was good. But it lacked the depth necessary to make it a good implementation plan.

After difficult negotiations relative to financing, the deal was finally closed in November. The company's owner told his consultant to expect an invitation to a February grand opening.

"Doesn't February sound a little quick?" the consultant asked the owner. "Shouldn't you sit down and draw up a more detailed implementation plan?" The owner had a lot of equipment to buy, personnel to hire, and marketing to do. Some city approvals were also required.

"Don't worry," the owner said. He felt he knew what he was doing.

The grand opening was held in May. It was beautiful, but it was also the company's last hurrah. The owner had planned to have $125,000 in working capital when the business opened. But after being delayed for four months, and after throwing the lavish party, he was practically tapped out.

The lesson here is that any time there is a dynamic situation, there should be a business plan. If there are unaccounted-for variables, they should at least be acknowledged and noted.

Exxon lost millions of dollars in the office products business. So did Digital Equipment Corp. in the personal computer business. Companies that size can survive debacles and go on to future successes, but small companies can't. They need to plan carefully.

SUCCEEDING BY SUCCEEDING, SUCCEEDING BY NOT FAILING

There are those who succeed by succeeding. They have some kind of "magic"—persistence, gumption, chutzpah, the willingness to roll the dice and the luck to have it come up seven—that can't be taught; or if it can, it can only be taught over many years. Some people are almost destined to succeed because of past success. Entrepreneurs with track records of success get

significant attention paid to their plans, and often get the benefit of the doubt in organizing a venture.

Although succeeding by succeeding can't be taught except
through years of experience, succeeding by not failing can be.
This, in many ways, is the heart of business planning.

There are a number of key hurdles in the creation of any
business, each of which can result in disaster if improperly addressed. These include developing management and support
employees, raising capital, developing and marketing product,

FIGURE 1–1. Succeeding by Not Failing (Half of the Formula for Success).

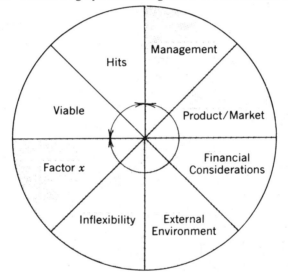

This chart reflects the relationship between business failure and success for
new enterprises. The shaded area reflects failure. This area is further divided into wedges which identify functional areas into which costly mistakes may be categorized. The three-to-one ratio of failure to success is
probably not far from reality. While each wedge in the shaded area is equal
in size and thus does not reflect a statistically accurate representation of
the proportion of failures attributable to a particular functional area, it is
instructive. To the extent that the entrepreneur addresses each functional
area in a way that reduces the probability of costly error, the odds increase
that the venture will be one of the fortunate ones that end up in the white
(success) area.

keeping margins acceptable, and dealing with outside influences. Depending on which statistics one uses, 75 percent of all new businesses fail in the first few years, most for one of these reasons. A few are attacked by "factor x," the unpredictable (see Figure 1–1).

At each one of these hurdles, an entrepreneur must examine the business, ask questions, and ferret out the possible problems. Each time a businessperson identifies a problem and solves it, he or she eliminates one more variable that can cause failure, and increases the chances of success.

Through careful planning, most problems can be solved. By doing careful planning and solving all the problems that *can* be solved, a businessperson can, in effect, stack the deck in favor of success.

LOOKING BACKWARD—THE BUSINESS PLAN AS A YARDSTICK

The constant updating of the business plan helps the plan fulfill its second major purpose, that of being a yardstick against which to measure the company's actual performance.

Last year's business plan can tell a company what strategy was effective or ineffective, and what implementation was effective or ineffective.

Simplicity is a virtue to the extent that it eases implementation. However, often what looked simple on paper when the previous business plan was being prepared became complex in implementation. Examining the business's actual performance against the business plan can identify strengths and weaknesses in the organization—sometimes relating to people—that separate strategy from effective implementation.

The financial section of the previous business plan can be used in an objective, concrete way, to monitor the business's performance. The financial projections made when the plan was drawn up became the basis for the budget under which the company tried to operate. Deviations from that budget point out areas where either necessary resources were misjudged or possibly controls were lax during the period the business plan embraced.

In addition to management, others will use the business plan as a monitoring tool. Financial sources, both lenders and investors, will note deviations between the plan and the company's actual performance; they will also ask why those deviations occurred. They may ask the question in a cordial manner, as part of a meeting to draw up the next business plan. Or they may ask the question as they are telling the businessperson to pack his or her bags and hand over the key to the rest-room door, pursuant to the terms of the lending or investing agreement.

This is one of the arguments against overly hyping a business in a business plan. Professionals—consultants, accountants, and lawyers who work with businesspeople in writing business plans and securing financing—often counsel their clients to make realistic projections. Why should an entrepreneur aspire to be "superhuman" and risk not meeting projections, when a little more modesty will produce projections that can much more easily be attained—or even exceeded—thereby keeping lenders happy and still providing investors with a healthy rate of return.

RAISING CASH—THE BUSINESS PLAN AS A FINANCING TOOL

This is the role of a business plan most people think of first. While we list this role last, it too is critical. After all, if a business can't raise cash, all else may be moot. Although raising cash is a critical hurdle, it is only the first of many.

Thinking that the primary role of a business plan is to be a sales tool to raise cash can get an entrepreneur into trouble. This emphasis can lead the businessperson to write a hyped-up plan that will not provide the objectivity necessary for the plan to fulfill its other two roles.

It is better to write an objective business plan and not get financing because the business is a bad risk than to have hypnotized oneself into thinking the risk is less. Hyped projections in a plan only present a sham—deliberately or not—to funding sources, the outcome of which is to have the house of cards come tumbling down later. Bankruptcy court as an end result is a risk to be strongly considered and avoided. It is in the area of raising cash that the business plan walks a fine line between an objective analysis of a company's future and a sales document.

In addition to being clear and well organized, the business plan must be written at a level of complexity the reviewer will understand and in a style that shows the preparer's excitement with the potential business.

THE BUSINESS PLAN—A MORE GENERALIZED TOOL

During the 1980s and into the 1990s, the business plan really came of age. What was once seen as primarily a financing tool became, in effect, standard operating procedure for businesspeople entering all sorts of business situations.

Business plans with the basic format described in this book are developed when a company is buying or expanding—whether the company is seeking outside financing or generating the capital from its own activities; downsizing, reorganizing, or selling.

The business plan format has become a common language, the structure around which businesspeople define and describe an entity's activities and determine if they have done the proper analysis of the business' potential. Depending on the circumstances, the tone of the business plan may be different, but the content will be basically the same.

A business plan's reviewers—whether it is the board of directors, a potential financing source, or a bankruptcy judge—must believe that the business can do what the plan states it will do.

USING PROFESSIONALS

Although we believe the business plan should always be prepared by the businessperson, it can be helpful to have professional input in the process from accountants, consultants, and/or lawyers. Informal sources of guidance—mentors, advisors, and the like—can also be valuable. Often these professionals will ask objective questions of an entrepreneur and a plan that the businessperson has not yet explored, either because he or she just didn't think of it or because the answer seemed intuitively obvious. Professionals can often point out missing information or the magnitude of problems that may seem small to the entrepreneur, tone down claims that may be overblown or misleading, or help the entrepreneur clarify points in the plan.

Reviewers go through a process known as "due diligence"—an in-depth evaluation—before lending or investing money in a project. Preparers should, in effect, go through the same process, and professionals can often be catalysts in this process. Gaps and flaws in the plan should be addressed. Questions reviewers will ask should be asked and, if possible, answered in the business plan itself before the reviewers see it. If a question is posed in the plan (or by the reviewer) that can't be answered immediately, this should be admitted in the plan.

An example of the kind of give-and-take that can go on between entrepreneurs and professionals is a pair of entrepreneurs whose retail store sells only compact disks (CDs) to music listeners. The entrepreneurs were looking for funding to expand to other locations. The first question asked by the consultant who was hired to help them raise money was, "How do you know you can replicate your success in other locations?"

After they convinced him they could do it again, they told him they wanted to open 15 stores in 15 separate markets. The entrepreneurs believed there was a window of opportunity in the then-new CD market and they wanted to be the first CD-only store in a number of markets. The consultant pointed out three major difficulties in having 15 stores in as many markets: they would be difficult to manage; it would be difficult to get to know the dynamics of 15 local markets; and there would be a loss of economy of scale with regard to advertising.

Today, as we know, these kinds of issues have often been overcome. Regional and even national chains of CD, video and other home entertainment stores have prospered either as company-owned or franchise locations.

The consultant suggested trying to saturate a narrower regional market with five to eight stores first, to further gauge whether the CD-only idea would really work outside the immediate area. The entrepreneurs convinced him that this was not a large enough market at that time to support so many stores.

They settled on a plan initially to put 10 stores in three areas—and then to expand into the other 12 cities over a few years. The entrepreneurs had realistic projections; it was just a matter of finding out how best to reach those numbers.

Some entrepreneurs come to us expecting to make millions on businesses that obviously aren't conceptually good enough. We've seen literally thousands of plans. No one ever writes a business plan saying he or she is going to fail. It's always a question of how much money they are going to make, and how fast it is going to happen. Younger, less experienced businesspeople often believe they will make more money than older entrepreneurs who have been around the track a few times.

They often generate ideas that are derivative, not realizing that windows of opportunity open and close rapidly. If the all-CD concept was bold in the mid-1980s and a consultant urged caution, the same consultant would welcome a similar proposal today by saying "What's new? How do you expect to beat the established regional and/or national chains?" Conventional wisdom advocates being conservative in projections.

Writing the business plan is not a formidable task if an entrepreneur truly understands his or her venture. Much of the information is either at the entrepreneur's disposal, within easy researching distance, or intuitively obvious. However, determining the comparative worth of all of the information and organizing it in the best way is challenging, and is usually improved by at least a cursory glance from an unbiased professional.

THE ROLE OF THE PLAN IN RAISING MONEY

Since most business plans are written by people looking for financing, the plan's ultimate test is how much interest it can generate from reviewers in as little time as possible. In this regard, it is important to understand that the business plan is really only the beginning of the money-raising process. It is the first in a series of documents a reviewer will receive.

If it conveys in a clear, readable, and digestible form the company's basic goals and methods, a reviewer will pay attention. If they want more information, reviewers are not shy about asking for more detail.

A plan for a computer software development company should not necessarily have 40 pages of code in it, but it should have a sentence saying that 40 pages of code are available for inspection should the reviewer or his or her designated technical expert want to see them.

The plan should be used as a negotiating tool. When preparing a plan, an entrepreneur should be specific about what he or she wants from the lender or investor, but vague about what he or she is willing to give up. This puts the ball in the investor's or lender's court. By holding back a card or two, without being misleading, the entrepreneur will allow the reviewer to establish the first negotiating point.

Remember, finally, that the business plan is a confidential document. It should be distributed only to those who have a need to see it, such as members of the management team, professional advisors, and potential sources of money. Confidentiality forms such as the sample in Chapter 14 should be signed by those who receive copies of the plan. There is no reason to produce a large quantity of copies. Nor is there a reason to produce glossy, bound volumes.

First, this would make it difficult and expensive to update. Second, it would imply that many people were seeing the plan. Sources of financing often get a queasy feeling if they think a plan is being "shopped around." We suggest that a plan initially be sent to at least 3 but fewer than 10 possible sources of financing. Plans should never be sent to professional sources sequentially, with the entrepreneur waiting for a reply from each before moving to the next. This approach could postpone a success for years.

When determining who to send a plan to, entrepreneurs should carefully research what kind of sources are interested in the field they are in; some banks only lend in certain geographic areas, some investors only invest in certain types of businesses. Second, within a given organization, there may be a number of people or departments that can deal with business plans. They may also be divided geographically, by business group, or in another way. It is important to get a plan to the right group and ideally to the proper person.

In Chapter 2, we'll talk more about who these people are and what they're looking for when they examine a business plan.

2

WHO READS THE BUSINESS PLAN?

WHAT ARE THEY LOOKING FOR? HOW DO THEY MAKE FUNDING DECISIONS?

The business plan will be read by people both inside and outside the company. Inside readers will usually be limited to the management team and the board of directors.

Outside readers will mostly be those who are sources of funding, although professional advisors will read the plan, and occasionally even a supplier, distributor, or others who have a business interest in the company may want to read it in order to understand how the company runs so he or she can better serve it. For this chapter, however, we will concentrate on those who read the business plan in the context of potentially financing the business.

In general, there are two types of funding sources: lenders and investors. The lenders we are generally referring to are commercial banks, corporate finance companies and investment bankers.

When lenders consider a loan request, they concentrate on what are sometimes referred to as the "four Cs" of credit: character, cash flow, collateral, and (equity) contribution.

Investors look at many of the same factors, although they often weigh the factors differently and even define them differently. This is because lenders and investors are looking for different things in a business they fund.

Lenders are looking for the ability of a company to repay its debt. No matter how big a hit a company is, usually a lender has only the promise of being rewarded with steady payments of principal and interest. While a borrower may become a better customer as the business becomes larger, the bank or finance company will not necessarily prosper in direct proportion to the company's success.

On the other hand, investors enjoy the possibility of a large rate of return, since they have a "piece of the action" (an equity position) in a company in return for their investment. Consequently, they are willing to accept more risk.

LENDING AND THE FOUR Cs

Character

Character is a crucial element in an individual's or a company's attempt to secure a loan. "Character" is of course a subjective, "soft" criterion that enters into the lender's decision process. Nonetheless, the lender must have confidence in the individual he or she is dealing with or the lender won't go forward with the venture. Such traits as talent, reliability, and honesty come rolling off the tongues of bankers as they try to describe character.

One slice of character that stands up to objective measure, and is therefore always used by lenders, is credit history. Make no mistake about it though, credit history in terms of a commercial loan is a one-way street. A bad credit rating will often knock a potential new business out of the credit-obtaining box. A good credit history on the other hand will do little on the positive side. Just because an individual pays his or her Bloomingdale's credit card obligation each month does not mean he or she would be good at running a business.

In the final analysis, even with the objective credit history, a lender's decision comes down to intuition: How capable is this individual? Will he or she run the business ethically and keep us honestly appraised of the real status of the business? How much faith can we have that this individual can successfully run a business and pay the debt service?

Cash Flow

Lenders need to be satisfied that cash flow will be adequate to cover debt service throughout the term of the obligation. Most loans are structured with interest payments due every month beginning in month one, and principal payments also due usually beginning in month one. In some instances principal payments can be deferred, but usually no more than one year.

To satisfy lenders the business must be strong enough to meet debt service and operating obligations, and still have enough available cash to provide a comfortable cushion in order to address uncertainties. Entrepreneurs must remember that projections are imperfect and must therefore provide for deviations. Lenders will want to be assured that the margin for error has been considered and provided for.

Effectively projecting cash flow requires sound judgment and intuition. However, the entrepreneur should project cash flow with a sensitivity to industry norms and standards, and should give a logical explanation if the plan shows a projected departure from these norms.

Collateral

No good lender will make a decision to loan money based solely on strong collateral. But every good lender will try to get the best collateral possible on a loan. This normally involves securing the lender's interest by liens or mortgages against tangible assets—such as real estate or equipment. In addition, most lenders will require the entrepreneur's personal signature, both as additional security and as evidence of the borrower's real commitment to the venture.

As an example of how pervasive it is for lenders to require personal signatures of small businesspeople, a consultant once asked a commercial lender when she would *not* demand a personal signature on a note. Her reply was: "When your client can't write."

Now is as good a time as any to destroy the *myth of limited liability* as it relates to the debts of small incorporated businesses. Many new businesspeople believe that because their business is incorporated, their personal assets are not in jeopardy. While this may be true of unsecured creditors such as suppliers, commercial lenders will "pierce the corporate veil" by insisting on personal signatures. Because of this, the risks in such a borrowing relationship will be high.

However, there are some strategies to minimize personal liability if the deal turns sour. These will allow the entrepreneur to go further up the reward ladder without climbing so far out on the risk limb.

As an example, one may keep personal assets in the name of other family members, most often a spouse or child. Also, assets held jointly by spouses cannot be taken by a lender unless the lender has both spouses' signatures on the note. Incidentally, most lenders will ask for both signatures if collateral is otherwise insufficient.

The issues related to personal liability and loan repayment are complex, and it is often important to have advice from a lawyer when making borrowing arrangements. We will discuss some of these issues in greater detail in Chapter 3.

Contribution

Lenders' requirements vary as to the amount of personal equity contribution they want an entrepreneur to have in the business. However, almost all lenders require a significant commitment of both time and money by an entrepreneur. This helps ensure that the entrepreneur is closely tied to the company's success and therefore the success of the financing. It also serves to reduce the lender's exposure relative to the deal's total size. This provides a cushion to allow the lender to come out "whole" in the event of a default.

In addition, different industries customarily have different ratios of debt to equity, commonly known as leverage. Some industries have traditionally been highly leveraged, with debt three to four times greater than equity, often because of high success rates and/or generally good-quality collateral. Real estate and the apparel industries are good examples of highly leveraged businesses. An unusually high failure rate and/or poor-quality collateral may result in relatively low leverage in an industry, as exemplified by the restaurant business. Because of these vagaries it is difficult to generalize as to how much the entrepreneur must contribute to a venture.

TERMS OF DEBT

Repayment Period

The repayment period—the length of time over which the obligation is amortized (paid off)—usually depends on the useful life of the asset financed, although there can be some variance. If a lender really wants to make a deal, he or she can give some latitude in order to structure the debt so that the deal makes sense economically and cash flow is sufficient to amortize the debt. Working capital loans are usually paid off over the shortest periods of time and real estate loans over the longest. Remember, the longer the term is, the lower the monthly payment—principal and interest—will be, but there will be more monthly payments, more interest accruing, and more money paid in total to meet the debt requirements.

Many lenders are willing to give initial moratoriums on principal payments—periods of time at the beginning of a loan when only interest is due. Often these will be allowed during periods of start-up or expansion, when a business is incurring expenses in excess of revenues. It is possible that an enlightened lender will extend such a moratorium up to 12 months.

Less frequently, but still possible, longer moratoriums may be given by the lender to help a company through some hard times. However, except in very rare instances, there are no moratoriums on interest payments. Failure to meet interest payment typically constitutes a loan default. Normally, on default, the entire principal amount outstanding becomes immediately due.

Rates

Most business debt today is provided at a variable interest rate, usually fluctuating with the prime rate (the rate banks charge their "best" customers). This rate is usually quoted as "prime plus" x percentage points, often .5 percent to 2 percent, but it can be as much as 3 or even 4 percent above prime depending on risk and other variables that motivate the lender. The effective rate changes as often as the prime rate changes, therefore each monthly payment can be different.

Variable-rate debt has become prevalent since the late 1970s, when interest rates were volatile and commercial lenders decided that they would pass this volatility on to the borrower rather than absorbing it in their fixed-rate loan portfolio.

There will, no doubt, be a host of other covenants, rules, and restrictions to the loan, which restrict an entrepreneur's freedom of management to such an extent for example, he or she may not give raises to senior management without the lender's approval, or may not obtain further financing without the lender's approval.

To generalize about the difference between lenders and investors, lenders are more numbers-driven in their analyses of a business's potential, and more short-sighted in that they focus on the first couple of years of a business's life, when viability, rather than potential, is likely to be achieved. They will require that cash flow is sufficient to service the debt, and will often concentrate on the downside more than the possible upside of the business. This is due to their reward structure. Unlike investors, lenders are not involved with a business for a piece of the action.

One of the major advantages of financing a business with debt instead of investment is that lenders often make decisions faster than investors. It is not outrageous to expect some decisions from lenders and even a closing on financing within two to three months of the time the lender first sees the business plan. With venture capitalists, this time is often doubled or even tripled. (These time frames assume an "arm's-length" relationship, where entrepreneurs and financing sources don't already know each other.)

INVESTORS

For the most part, in this section, we will focus on venture capitalists. There are a number of other important sources of equity financing, however, which we will discuss later. Many people who write business plans, in fact, write them with venture capitalists in mind.

When people think of venture capitalists, they normally are thinking about the professional venture-capital fund managers who make the decisions about which companies a fund should invest in. Typically these people are looking for young, high-growth "operating" companies—companies that are ongoing rather than "one-shot deals"—or real estate development.

The original venture capitalists, wealthy individuals or groups who aren't directly associated with a formal fund, are still the biggest part of the venture funding community. While the available funding for "venture capital" fluctuates from economic cycle to economic cycle, so-called angels continue to fund companies in the start-up and early-round financing phases.

Investors will often give more intense scrutiny when looking at a potential entrepreneur's character than lenders will. Part of this is based on the fact that they do fewer deals and have more time to do background checks. Some investors with entrepreneurial background develop a "sixth sense" about entrepreneurial character.

THE VENTURE CAPITAL FUND

Venture capital funds are usually set up as limited partnerships, with the professional manager being the general or controlling partner. He or she—or the management company—usually puts up a very small amount of the fund's capital, often as little as one percent. The rest of the fund is financed by limited partners, who put their money at risk and can get great rewards, but have no say in the fund's day-to-day management.

Most of these limited partners are financial institutions, pension funds, and corporations, although a few wealthy individual investors may be involved. Minimum participation is usually at least a few hundred thousand dollars, and can be over $1 million, which is why we see few individuals as limited partners in such funds.

Venture capitalists, whether funds or individuals, are mainly looking for two things:

- Rates of return of 25 to 50 percent or more compounded annually
- Investments that will become liquid within a relatively short period of time

The economics of a venture capital fund, which are somewhat peculiar, demand this. Venture funds have a defined lifetime, usually between 8 and 13 years. Within the first couple of years, the fund managers are sorting through hundreds of businesses looking for investment opportunities. Depending on the size of the fund and the number of managers in the venture management company, each venture fund may invest in as few as 10 or as many as 50 companies during its lifetime. Since venture capitalists like to keep a close watch on their investments, and have even been known to step in and run troubled companies on a day-to-day basis, they try not to spread their money or management too thin.

Venture capital often is an all-or-nothing game. In order for a fund to have a 25- or even a 50-percent annually compounded return for its lifetime—not unheard of at all—it must find one or two big successes in order to meet its return objectives after absorbing the impact of companies that either go bust or fail to achieve anticipated profitability.

Every fund hopes for a Federal Express or an Apple Computer or a Lotus Development Corp.—a company that will generate enormous returns—to offset their other investments that experience a more pedestrian business history.

Liquidity is very important, because at the end of the venture capital fund's defined lifetime the fund must be split up and returned to the investors. If a company is still privately held, its shares are not marketable and hence not convenient for this distribution. Venture capitalists' investments usually become liquid by either "going public"—that is, selling stock in its companies to the public—or by selling its interest in companies to another company. Such sales usually result in the fund receiving cash or marketable securities in a public company.

Venture capital managers have a much different system of compensation from that of lenders, and hence, are looking for different qualities in their investments. Fund managers receive an annual management fee—usually 2 or 3 percent of the total assets under management. In addition, at the time of distribution they receive a disproportionate amount, often 20 percent, of the total fund profits after the return of the initial capital to investors.

Some of the qualities venture capitalists associate with companies that have the potential to generate exciting returns are:

- *The Quality of the Individual Entrepreneur.* They are most often looking for maturity and experience in the area of other businesses started, along with a track record of success. What defines a quality entrepreneur for a venture capitalist is subjective and the evaluation is often intuitive.

- *Functionally Balanced Teams.* More and more, venture capitalists are looking for entrepreneurial teams that meet the human resource needs of a new company. Venture capital managers have little time to devote to helping structure management teams and oversee day-to-day operations. Hence the one-man show is less attractive than the professional and aggressive team.

- *Proprietary Characteristics.* Venture capitalists are always looking for businesses that have an edge on the competition that cannot easily be copied. Proprietary characteristics are often marked by patents, licenses, trademarks, or other legal protections.

Many venture capital funds also have special preferences for the type of business they will fund or the size of the investment they desire. Some provide "seed" money for rank start-ups, while others like to make larger second- or third-round financings to participate with businesses that already have a track record, albeit a short one. Such sources as *Who's Who in Venture Capital*, published by Wiley-Interscience, and the *Venture Capital Journal*, published by Venture Economics, can help entrepreneurs find these people.

Venture capitalists are often less sensitive to the issue of collateral than lenders. Because the promise of reward is so great, they are more willing to accept greater risk. Similarly, they want to see a contribution by the entrepreneur as evidence of his or her commitment. But they are not bound by ratios to the extent lenders are. Rather, venture capitalists usually look for a commitment that is in line with the resources of the entrepreneur.

Typically, venture capitalists will ask for at least one seat on the board of directors. Few like to take day-to-day control of a company, but most will do so if they are in danger of losing their investment. Many venture capital agreements have a formal mechanism for removing the entrepreneur if things aren't going well, while other venture capitalists will depend on their power and position on the board of directors to try to change company management if necessary.

A smooth progression of a financing from a venture capitalist might look something like the following timetable, which would hold for a company that has a fully written business plan, a well-defined strategy, intact management team, and some easy-to-reach references.

For four to six weeks, an entrepreneur is developing a business plan, and, simultaneously, identifying the appropriate funding sources. Then:

- *Weeks 1–2.* Initial contact with potential financing sources by letter or phone
- *Week 3.* Mailing of executive summary or complete plan
- *Weeks 4–6.* An initial meeting with one or more potential financing sources
- *Weeks 7–18.* Follow-up with one or more financing sources. Meetings, phone calls, additional information, or addenda to business plan
- *Week 18.* An offer from a financing source
- *Weeks 19–26.* Negotiation of the deal terms, drawing up of documents
- *Week 26.* Closing

OTHER FINANCING SOURCES

Self, Family, and Friends

Despite the popular conception, most initial investment in new businesses is not made by venture capitalists. It is made by a number of investors who are at less than an arm's length from the entrepreneur. Friends and family often supplement the entrepreneur's own capital.

These investments can be profitable for the investors and can have the advantage to the entrepreneur of a faster closing. However, since these investors are not "professionals" they tend to use less "due diligence" in their analyses of potential investments. This may result in their not evaluating a potential business on its objective merit, and making investment decisions that could in turn have a negative impact on personal relationships. The entrepreneur must consider this potential result before pursuing such investments.

By far the most frequent investor in new businesses is the entrepreneur and immediate family. The investment may come from savings, or other assets such as marketable securities, or equity in a home perhaps via a second mortgage.

For many small entrepreneurs, these are the most likely sources of financing for a business initially, since it is very difficult to get a commercial loan under $10,000 or $20,000, and even more difficult to get venture capital funding of less than $250,000.

Some people find even more "creative" ways of finding liquid assets with which to invest in their own new business. One example of a creative self-financing involved a man who wanted to start a specialty butcher shop. He had $10,000 and needed another $10,000. His friend, a small-business consultant, told him that it would be a tough sum to raise. A few weeks later, the butcher called and invited his friend to his new shop. "Where did you raise the money?" the consultant asked. "I sold my wife's Corvette," his friend replied. This was not an exotic, high-finance source of funding, but it was inventive and effective (one might wonder whether his wife thought this was inventive and effective).

A few entrepreneurs without a house to refinance or a sports car to sell have even turned to "plastic financing" to start a business. These people have gone to a number of banks, acquired credit cards, then borrowed to their financing limit on all of their cards, either taking cash or using the cards to buy supplies. This is a terribly expensive way to finance a deal and certainly not one we would recommend—most credit cards have rates of between 15 and 20 percent on unpaid balances—but for those who need small amounts and have little or no assets, there sometimes just isn't any other way.

"Angels"

Beyond digging into one's own pocket or the pockets of family and friends—which always risks more than just money—there is a network of informal investors (sometimes called angels) who are willing to put their money into new businesses. Some don't have enough funds to get into a venture capital fund but still like the risk of venture-type investments. Others like to take a more hands-on approach to their investment decisions. A few may even be gizmo-driven dilettantes looking for the next Rube Goldberg-type invention.

These people go through a review process, but it is often a limited review, and they usually make decisions much faster than professional venture capitalists—often in two to three months or less. The entrepreneur does not necessarily have to show these people the opportunity for the company to be an enormous hit, but he or she must show the investor that the money will return more than the investor could get with other less risky types of investments. This often means showing the possibility of the business giving at least a 20 percent or more compounded annual return on investment.

Another nice thing about working with these informal investors is that the deal can be structured any way the entrepreneur, the investor, and their respective lawyers wish to structure it. There can be a combination of debt and equity in such deals.

Informal investors can be found in a number of ways. Many of them hang around venture capital clubs, often breakfast clubs that meet in major cities. Another good way to find them is through professionals—lawyers, accountants, consultants, and financial planners.

In reality, any person or institution with a dollar to invest or lend is a potential source of financing. The entrepreneur must be a good detective, to identify the appropriate financing source for a potential business.

Each potential financing source has its own agenda for success and its own criteria for investing. Capital markets are imperfect, and there is no guarantee that an appropriate deal and financing source can be matched. It takes determination, persistence, and a strategy planned in advance by the entrepreneur to find the right source.

A few of the less well-known sources of financing are:

Vendors

One of the most overlooked sources for helping to finance a new venture is the vendors who do business with a company. If an entrepreneur can convince vendors to extend an extra 30 or 60 days' credit on accounts payable, this will greatly alleviate potential cash crunches and reduce capital requirements.

Corporate Venture Capitalists

A number of large companies have set up their own venture capital funds. Often, these funds are looking to help finance companies that can contribute technology to their company, or are in some other way compatible. Sometimes the corporate venture company is even looking for entrepreneurs to spawn companies the larger company will eventually acquire.

Ad-Hoc Venture Pools

Some private investors have banded together to form informal investment groups or investment pools. Often one private money source will turn to other private investors to get the money together to make an investment in a venture.

The Small Business Investment Corporation (SBIC) and Minority Enterprise Small Business Investment Corporation

(MESBIC) are companies that have investment pools of private money that are leveraged with federal government funds via the Small Business Administration.

Economic development groups, sometimes called "economic development corporations" or "business development corporations," administered on a federal, state, or local level, may provide either favorably structured debt or equity. These organizations try to make responsible investment and lending decisions, but because they lack the profit motive are more benevolent in structuring a deal than other funding sources.

While the majority of these were federally funded in the 1970s and into the 1980s, today the economic development torch has passed to the states, many of which will invest capital, loan money, or guarantee loans as well as defer taxes due, pay for training, or offer other incentives to entrepreneurs willing to create jobs in their state.

Some private foundations and universities put a small percentage of their endowment portfolios into small, risky ventures. Some foundations even make cash grants for development projects, if the venture dovetails with their own goals.

There are even a few mutual funds that invest in start-up and small, growth-oriented companies. These are, in effect, venture capital funds for small investors who want a little of their money invested in high-risk ventures.

An extreme example of benevolence is seen in the Small Business Innovation Research program. Under this federal program, grants are awarded on a competitive basis. There is no obligation to pay the grants back. They are awarded based on the appeal of the company's technology. First-round grants of up to $50,000 and second-round grants of up to $500,000 are awarded by federally sponsored programs.

3

THE BUSINESS'
LEGAL FORM

Choosing the legal form under which a business will operate is one of the more complex and critical decisions an entrepreneur must make when organizing a new business. This chapter outlines some of the more common alternative legal forms of business organization and the various reasons for organizing a business in any particular way. The information is not all inclusive; indeed, whole books have been written on the subject. The question of legal form is one that should be studied carefully by an entrepreneur, working in close consultation with a lawyer and tax accountant.

MAJOR VARIABLES

The three major variables an entrepreneur must deal with when choosing the legal form of a business are:

1. Liability
2. Control
3. Taxes

In general, all businesses are organized as sole proprietorships, partnerships, or corporations. There are variations possible within these designations. Limited partnerships offer partners some very specific benefits; special corporations known as S corporations (formerly known as subchapter S corporations) offer shareholders other special benefits. All of these options should be evaluated.

Before examining the various legal forms, the answers to the following questions should be known:

- Will the entrepreneur be the sole owner? If not, how many other people—either operators or investors—will have an ownership interest? How much control will each owner have? In what manner will the risks and rewards of the business be shared?

- How important is it for all owners to limit personal liability for debts or claims against the business?

- Which form of business organization affords the most advantageous tax treatment for both the business and the individual owner(s)?

- What legal form will be the simplest and least expensive, both to establish and to maintain?

- What are the business' long-term plans?

Sometimes the answers to these questions will conflict with one another. At this point professional assistance by lawyers and accountants can help sort out the issues. However, the entrepreneur should be mindful of the following:

1. Legal forms of business were established for *legal* reasons, meaning that liability issues were paramount to those who wrote the earliest laws regarding business. Corporate taxation is a relatively recent phenomenon and has become an important and complex issue only over the past half century. Taxes should have an impact on, but not necessarily dictate, the decision as to the legal form.

2. Simplicity should not be underestimated. A simple organizational form, which often costs little or nothing to

establish and maintain, can often save more than would be saved in taxes by a more complicated legal form. This is especially true for a small business.

3. The U.S. tax laws constantly change. This chapter is based on the Internal Revenue Code of 1986 as amended through December, 1992. In 1986, the overhaul of the tax system that started with the election of President Ronald Reagan in 1980 was culminated. During the Reagan Administration, Congress passed eight major pieces of tax legislation.

After passage of the Tax Reform Act of 1986, Congress hinted that there would be no significant tax law changes for several years. Nevertheless, tax bills were passed in 1987, 1988, and 1990. Some 1987 changes reversed 1986 actions.

As this edition is being written, Congress continues to make tax law changes. Many of these changes "fine tune" the tax laws and raise revenues to pay for new programs. However, studies are also underway involving larger issues, such as a way to end double taxation of corporate profits and the imposition of a national sales tax or value-added tax (VAT). Though corporate America has complained repeatedly to Congress that tax planning needs a longer horizon of certainty to be effective, Congress has not curbed its appetite for tax-law changes.

With this as background, let's review the alternative forms of organizing a business.

SOLE PROPRIETORSHIPS

The sole proprietorship provides a businessperson with the maximum in simplicity and flexibility, while trading off all protection against personal liability. It also affords the business' owner complete control. Once other owners become involved, a sole proprietorship is no longer possible.

An individual who wants to establish a sole proprietorship usually goes through very few formalities on the state level, the most onerous being a simple registration of the business under the Fictitious Names Act. On the federal level, the sole proprietor needs only to keep accurate accounting records and file a Schedule C (Profit or Loss from a Business or Profession) as an attachment to IRS Form 1040 at the appropriate tax time. Sole proprietorships must operate on a calendar year, but can use either the cash or accrual method of accounting (the accrual method may be mandatory if the business has inventories).

A sole proprietorship does not separate the individual from his or her business. This is advantageous in that the individual can commingle funds (although a separate bank account is preferable); remove assets from the business with few, if any, legal or tax consequences; and, provided he or she "materially participates" in the business and is "at risk" for monies lost, use any or all of the loss from the sole proprietorship to offset taxable income earned from other sources, including regular earned income.

However, this lack of separation means that it is difficult within a sole proprietorship for the entrepreneur to limit his or her personal liability against debt payment. Legal liability for defective products, professional malpractice, or any other claims will also be a personal liability. However, the business can be guarded against these liabilities by insurance, as with any business.

The tax advantages and disadvantages of sole proprietorships are becoming increasingly hard to discern. Until 1982, payroll taxes were an advantage, since the sole proprietor paid only 75 percent of the combined employer and employee share of the federal employment tax on his or her income. Since 1982, sole proprietors have gradually reached "parity" in social security payments, paying both the employer's and employee's shares. If the entrepreneur is still employed elsewhere, the social security taxes paid on his wages offset the social security taxes due on any self-employment income, although a self-employment loss will not offset social security taxes due from other earned income.

Sole proprietors do not pay social security taxes on compensation paid to spouses or minor children who work for the business. In addition, they pay no unemployment tax for the owner, unlike other legal forms in which unemployment taxes are paid for owner/employees.

A significant disadvantage of sole proprietorship is that the proprietor cannot get federal tax deductions for the cost of group term life, medical, and disability insurance coverage that inures to the benefit of the sole proprietor. In a corporation, an owner/employee gets federal tax deductions for these expenses. A technique for gaining the medical benefit is to put the spouse to work and have the family medical coverage go to him or her as an employee.

Self-employed individuals, including sole proprietors, are allowed a deduction of 25 percent of medical insurance premiums when computing adjusted gross income, although Congress has considered either increasing the deduction to 100 percent or, at the other extreme, eliminating it altogether.

One way to minimize the total tax burden to the sole proprietor in the past was to incorporate the business at a point when the marginal rate of the individual exceeded the corporate tax rate. But the Tax Reform Act of 1986 (TRA '86) changed rates so that for the first time corporate rates are always higher than individual tax rates. This leaves almost no reason for single-owner businesses to incorporate for tax-saving reasons. Unless you have a compelling business reason to incorporate, it is now usually advantageous to operate as a sole proprietor. But if incorporation serves other business interests, you may be able to achieve the tax benefits of sole proprietorship within corporate parameters by operating as an S corporation.

PARTNERSHIPS

Partnerships have many of the same features, both advantageous and disadvantageous, as sole proprietorships, except that there is more than one owner. A partnership can be relatively simple and informal, and requires minimal paperwork for state and federal authorities in order to be established. However, it is always a good idea for partners to have some form of written agreement about how they will share in the obligations, profits or losses, or capital of the partnership. Without a partnership agreement, state laws will generally dictate the allocation of such items.

Partnership agreements can include any items the partners think worthwhile to include. Some partnerships, especially limited partnerships set up for investment purposes, have a defined lifetime. How a partner joins or leaves the partnership, rights of interest purchase by other partners, terms of payment, and other such issues should be considered when drawing up partnership agreements.

Because partnerships legally dissolve on the death of any partner who owns more than a 10 percent interest, it is important to consider how the partnership can be least disrupted by this event. The right of surviving partners to buy out the deceased partner's spouse or other family members, often using the proceeds from "key person" insurance, is one way many partnerships cover themselves against this eventuality.

Partners do not take a salary as such, although many draw cash against their ultimate share of the profits. Each partner must include a statement of the partnership's income, losses, deductions, and/or credits on his or her federal income tax return (Form 1040). Because partners' cash income is not a salary, there is no tax withheld by the partnership and each partner must pay self-employment as if he or she were a sole proprietor. Partners do not pay unemployment taxes. In addition, because no income taxes are withheld from draws or earnings distributions, estimated tax payments must be made quarterly by each partner for federal and state purposes. Sole proprietors are subject to the same rules.

The big advantage of partnerships is the ease of getting assets into and out of a multiple-owner business without incurring taxes. This is important if investors are contributing more than money to a venture. As with sole proprietors, partners cannot take advantage of the tax deductability of the cost of their personal group term life, health, and disability insurance coverage (they may take the same 25 percent deduction for health insurance as sole proprietors).

As with sole proprietorships, the tax advantages of incorporating were almost nullified by TRA '86. Despite this, good business reasons should not prevent a partnership from incorporating. However, an S corporation form of business, discussed later, may offer most of the tax advantages of a partnership with the legal advantages of a corporation.

LIMITED PARTNERSHIPS

When partners need more money than they can put into a venture themselves and either cannot or do not want to borrow, they turn to a method of organization known as a *limited partnership*. A limited partnership offers certain partners who agree to become general partners a chance to raise capital from others while keeping control over the venture. Investors—known as limited partners—have the opportunity to own an equity position while limiting their liability and involvement in the venture to a financial one. Limited partners have no say in how a business operates and are only financially liable up to the amount of their investment. The general partners manage the business and have full exposure to liability. Sometimes, the general partners will be special-purpose corporations so that the liability issue can be managed.

With limitations on control, limited partnerships tend to be asset-based and in the past tended to be tax-advantaged for the investor. While TRA '86 put a severe limitation on the ability of a limited partner to draw tax advantages from investments in a limited partnership, with attractive rates of return and economic substance, the limited partnership structure can still be a viable option to an entrepreneur's capital raising needs.

S corporations, which from a tax posture are very similar to limited partnerships, are limited to no more than 35 shareholders, with restrictions against those shareholders being foreigners and corporations. Limited partnerships do not have these restrictions and hence may offer the advantages of limiting the liability of investors with no limit on the number or type of investors.

Another advantage limited partnerships have over S corporations is that in an S corporation all shares must have equal attributes, meaning one share must have the same benefits and
liabilities as any other. In limited partnerships, the shares of
general partners can have attributes not given to limited partners, such as control and a variable allocation percentage for
performance-based partnership distributions to the general
versus limited partners.

Venture capital funds are set up as limited partnerships, for
example, so that the fund managers, who act as general partners, can put up little capital and get a hefty return when the
fund is dissolved, in return for his or her expertise in managing the fund over its lifetime.

Other drawbacks to limited partnerships include the lack of
secondary markets and more difficult transferability of ownership compared with shares of corporations.

CORPORATIONS

Although most people think of corporations when they think
of businesses, in reality only a small percentage of American
businesses are formally incorporated. Incorporating can be a
costly and time-consuming process. State incorporation fees
and legal fees for drawing up corporate documents can easily
cost hundreds or thousands of dollars, and there are ongoing
expenses to maintaining and operating a corporation.

Businesses are incorporated most often for the benefits of
limited liability. In a corporation, owners, officers, and directors are not usually personally liable for the company's debts
(officers responsible for making employment-withholding tax
payments to the federal government can be held personally liable if those payments are not made). However, as discussed
in Chapter 2 regarding bank loans, the "corporate veil" is often
pierced by a bank asking for a personal signature on a corporate loan. This will most often be required of small, single-
owner, or closely held corporations.

Corporations have unlimited lives and, in the event of the death of a shareholder, ownership is passed to the heirs designated by the shareholder. The corporate stock can always be sold to other investors. In this way, large blocks of voting stock or even controlling interest can pass from owners who have employment or entrepreneurial stakes in the business (or the heirs of these people) to new owners.

Corporations have the flip-side relationship to employment and unemployment taxes as do sole proprietorships and partnerships. The corporation ultimately pays 100 percent of the employee/employer tax for all owner/employees (50 percent to the employee in cash as part of the salary—which is then withheld—and 50 percent directly to the government). In addition, corporations pay unemployment taxes for owner/employees. However, these tax payments are deductible for corporate income tax purposes.

Payments for group term life insurance premiums for policies up to $50,000 in death benefits are also deductible, as are payments for group disability and medical insurance. None of these benefits is taxable to employee/owners as income.

Since ownership of a corporation is marketable via shares of stock, it is possible to partially dispose of an ownership interest, although it is difficult to sell a holding in a closely held corporation. By contrast, one cannot sell an interest in a sole proprietorship, but only an interest in the proprietorship's underlying assets.

CORPORATIONS AND TAXES

Incorporating offers a number of federal income tax advantages. However, the government discourages incorporating merely for acquiring tax advantages.

One tax advantage comes from the ability of the owner/employee to control the allocation of income between corporate profits and individual salaries. This was more of an issue prior to 1986, when corporate and individual tax rates became more closely aligned. However, state taxes need to be considered as well as federal taxes. Pennsylvania, for example, has a 9 percentage point spread between corporate and individual tax rates.

Salary drawn can be controlled within limits of reasonableness. Too much salary could be challenged by the IRS as a disguised dividend and hence not be deductible to the corporation. Also, financing sources may put restrictions (primarily limitations) on salaries to owners, and severely limit the company's ability to pay dividends.

The "accumulated earnings tax" keeps both closely held and public corporations from retaining for use in the business more than $250,000 in earnings without justifiable reasons. Professional corporations such as doctors, lawyers, accountants, and consultants who often incorporate for the liability shield and tax advantages may retain only $150,000 before the accumulated earnings tax comes into consideration.

Cash accumulations for working capital, capital expansion, debt repayment, and other reasonable business needs may enable accumulated earnings to exceed the limit without triggering the tax. Corporations should have any expansion plans well documented before any IRS audit.

A corporation that plans to have a high ratio of dividend payout to net earnings will be penalizing its shareholders by having the pretax corporate income taxed at a combined effective tax rate of as high as 54.4 percent. Compare this to a sole proprietor's or partner's effective maximum tax rate of 31 percent.

Under prior tax laws, keeping the dividend payout to a minimum increased the inherent value of the corporation's stock. This inside buildup of undeclared dividends could then be cashed out at a later point in time via sale of stock and the gains thereon were taxed at significantly more favorable capital gains tax rates. However, the current tax law has removed most of the preferential tax treatment of capital gains, as well as making it more difficult if not impossible to avoid double taxation on a sale of corporate assets.

S CORPORATIONS

S corporations can offer entrepreneurs the best of both worlds in many ways. S corporations are not different from corporations under federal law and under some states' corporate laws. They offer owners the benefits of limited liability. In addition, there are usually no federal income taxes at the corporate level for S corporations. Profits or losses from S corporations flow directly through the company to the shareholders thereby avoiding double taxation. Investors are also able to use losses from S corporations as direct write-offs against other income, with limitations for those shareholders considered to be passive investors.

Because of this special tax treatment, for federal tax purposes, an S corporation is treated much like a partnership. However, there are limits on S corporations with regard to its ownership structure.

S corporations are allowed to have only one class of common stock (although it can have voting and non-voting stock), whereas regular corporations may have common stock, preferred stock, or other classes of stock. Generally, all S corporation stockholders must be U.S. citizens or resident aliens, and all must be individuals, special types of trusts, or estates. (These restrictions on ownership may make it difficult to offer stock to a lender or investor and still qualify as an S corporation. Phantom stock or warrants could be issued and the S election retained until the "shares" are actually converted into real shares.)

The S corporation cannot be part of an affiliated group of corporations, and a formal election has to be made with all the shareholders' consent to be taxed as an S corporation. Profits or losses are allocated to the shareholders on a per-share, per-day basis.

Once S status is lost because the business fails to qualify, or because shareholders vote for the company to revoke S status, the company cannot return to S status for five years unless permission is granted by the IRS. Inadvertently terminated S corporation elections may get relief from the IRS.

S corporation status is often chosen by entrepreneurs who feel the company will have losses in the first few years; losses can be passed directly through to investors who materially participate in the business as a tax shelter. Investors are allowed to deduct losses to the extent of the shareholder's investment in the stock and any loans to the corporation.

This can backfire if profits occur, since any income is also passed directly through to the shareholders and, if the company is successful, investors will have to report taxable income. If no cash distributions have occurred, they would have "income" on which to pay tax, without cash flow from the income. Many S corporations will distribute at least enough cash for the owners to pay their income tax related to the passed-through income. After all, if the company was a regular corporation, it would be paying its own taxes to the IRS.

Shareholders of at least 2 percent of the company's stock are treated as "partners" for purposes of taxation of fringe benefits. Because of this, 2 percent owner/employees of S corporations no longer enjoy the benefits of employees of corporations, such as tax-free group term life insurance, health, and disability insurance.

In many ways, S corporations provide the "best of both worlds" to entrepreneurs, however, the tax laws regarding S corporations are complex and the legal and accounting costs of starting and maintaining S status could override some of the tax advantages. State laws vary as to the taxability of an S corporation's income. Shareholders domiciled in a state other than that of the corporation may be subject to the individual income taxes of the corporation's domicile state.

The owners' effective tax rate on income from an S corporation never exceeds 31 percent (the maximum personal rate). However, for an individual operating in the form of a regular corporation, the effective tax depends on the level of that corporation's pretax income and the percentage of that corporation's net income paid out as cash dividends.

TABLE 3–1. Key Characteristics of Alternative Forms of Legal Organization

	Sole Proprietorship	Partnership	Limited Partnership	Corporation	S Corporation
Simplicity	Simplest and least expensive form to establish and maintain.	Relatively simple to establish and maintain. A written partnership agreement should be drawn up at the beginning.	More complex than simple partnership. Needs a formal written agreement. Many limited partnerships are marketable securities and must be registered, causing additional time and expense.	Generally requires the most formality in establishing and maintaining.	Same degree of formality and expense as a regular corporation to establish. Maintenance is more expensive because of the need for constant oversight.
Liability	Owner has unlimited personal liability.	Each partner has unlimited personal liability.	General partners are personally liable, while limited partners are only financially liable to the extent of their investment.	Stockholders not generally liable. In many small, closely held corporations, the owner or owners must personally cosign and guarantee loans. Corporate officers may also be liable for payment of withholding taxes.	Same.
Federal tax of profits	Owner taxed at individual rate.	Each partner is taxed at individual rates.	Partners are taxed at individual rates.	Taxed to corporation at corporate rates.	Shareholders are taxed at individual rates.
Deduction of losses (for investors "materially participating" in the business)	Yes.	Yes.	In certain circumstances.	No. Corporations carry over (back) losses, until they offset profits.	Yes.
Double taxation	No.	No.	No.	Yes.	No.

43

Corporations are taxed at a flat rate of 34 percent on all pretax income if it exceeds $335,000. Therefore, once this level is exceeded, there is rarely a point at which you are better off, taxwise, as a regular corporation.

However, if the corporation's pretax income is less than $50,000 and the owner does not intend to pay much in the way of cash dividends, total taxes may be less than 31 percent by doing business as a regular corporation.

Once the income level exceeds $50,000 and approaches $335,000, the benefit of lower corporate tax rates is gradually eliminated. Eventually you reach a point (approaching $335,000 of pretax income) where the effective tax rate that the owner pays will be greater than 31 percent even if dividends are not paid by the regular corporation. It is at this point that the owner is better off electing to do business as an S corporation.

Table 3–1 summarizes the key characteristics of the alternative forms of legal organization. These laws and tax rates are constantly changing, so determination of which form is best for your business should be made in close consultation with legal and tax advisors.

A FEW WORDS ABOUT BUYING A COMPANY

Buying an existing business involves many of the same legal and structural issues as starting a company, although often the purchaser has little ability to affect the legal form—at least in the short run.

If you make an asset acquisition the question is "what type of entity should make the purchase?" The entity could be a sole proprietorship, partnership, or corporation. If you purchase an existing company as a stock purchase, the corporation you buy will continue to survive.

But there are still choices: Will the acquiring entity be a corporation operating in a parent/subsidiary framework, or will you buy the stock directly? If so, will the acquired company change from a regular corporation to an S corporation?

A stock purchase involves assuming all a company's liabilities—both known and unknown—current and long-term. An asset purchase involves specific assets and the assumption of only designated liabilities.

In a stock acquisition, the purchase of a company involves the continuation of the company's tax history. If the business has had operating losses, these losses can be carried forward, with certain limitations under the 1986 tax laws.

These are complicated matters that can have long-term ramifications, so you should consult experts.

4

CONTENTS

A table of contents should be supplied for any business plan. It serves the same function as a table of contents for a book. It does not need to be detailed, or to show exactly the page where each section of the plan begins. On the contrary, new pages or sections may be added in updates, thus numbering could be a problem.

The business plan should be divided into sections, not chapters, although each section of a properly executed business plan corresponds to a chapter in this book.

GOOD FOODS, INCORPORATED
BUSINESS PLAN

Section:

Attachments to the Business Plan
14–1 Management Resumes
14–2 Competitive Analysis
14–3 Projection of Sales by Market Line
14–4 Product Line Profit Analysis
14–5 Sample Agreement of Confidentiality

5

EXECUTIVE SUMMARY

An executive summary is prepared for most business reports. Such a summary is particularly appropriate and often mandatory for a business plan.

An executive summary captures and presents succinctly the essence of the report. It is, in effect, a capsulized version of the entire plan. The executive summary is not simply a background statement, nor is it an introduction.

People who speak in public or write essays have long been taught to "tell 'em what you are going to tell 'em, tell 'em, then tell 'em what you just told 'em." The executive summary fulfills the first role—"telling 'em what you are going to tell 'em."

Many business plan reviewers are inundated with proposals. As a consequence, this summary must afford the reviewer a good first-cut understanding of the material. After reading an executive summary, a reviewer should have a relatively sound understanding of what will be presented in greater detail throughout the plan.

On occasion, the executive summary may be used by itself as a means of gaining access to a reader. Some venture capitalists prefer to review a cover letter and summary document prior to receiving a complete business plan.

While an executive summary appears at the beginning of the business plan, it should be written after the plan has been completed. It is only after the entire plan has been thought through and written that one is able to capsulize effectively and concisely.

There are a couple of major problems that come about when entrepreneurs try to write the executive summary before writing the rest of the business plan. One is that the executive summary will end up being vague and shallow, since the entire plan has not been thought through. The other is that the entrepreneur will often try to force the plan to conform to the "assumptions" or "statements" he or she makes in the executive summary.

In addition to facilitating a quick understanding of the proposal, an executive summary should get attention. Many venture capitalists, investors, and lenders indicate that it is not unusual to discard a proposal without reading beyond the executive summary. This is hardly surprising given that many of these individuals are faced with stacks of unsolicited business plans each day.

Thus the executive summary must succeed in generating immediate interest. The tone should be businesslike and should convey a sense of excitement and importance. The reviewer's interest might be captured by the concept, the rate of return, or even the style with which the thoughts are conveyed.

While this advice may seem to suggest drawing up a presentation that borders on the dramatic, one must be careful to present a concise, factual summary of the plan without being carried away with one's own hype.

A number of formats and approaches are appropriate for an executive summary. One that is often effective involves providing highlights of the business plan on a section-by-section basis. This begins with a few sentences or paragraphs that communicate the basic nature of the company and its current stage of development.

The executive summary then focuses on all or most functional areas, including a product profile, marketing plan, operational plan, and financial plan. The objective is to convey only the basic thoughts and highlights of each.

In the space of a few sentences or paragraphs, for example, a summary description of the financial plan might present the brief sales and profit history of an early-stage business, along with projected sales and profit performance. Other salient data, such as anticipated break-even points and return on equity, might also be provided. A review of such functional summaries together would give to reader an excellent feel for the detailed material that will follow.

It may be appropriate to conclude the executive summary on a personal note by offering a message from the principal(s). Again, this should be brief. It is intended to provide an opportunity to convey a personal assessment of the business's history to date (if there is one), and feelings about its future.

For example: "The founders of X, Y, Z Corp. are greatly encouraged by the immediate and enthusiastic acceptance by the market of our product line and believe that . . . "

Another option is to offer this sort of personal assessment in a cover letter accompanying the business plan.

II. EXECUTIVE SUMMARY

This business plan has been developed to present Good Foods, Incorporated (referred to as GFI or the company) to prospective investors and to assist in raising the $700,000 of equity capital needed to begin the sale of its initial products and finish development of its complete product line.

The Company

GFI is a start-up business with three principals presently involved in its development. The principal contact is Judith Appel of Nature's Best, Inc. (NBI), 24 Woodland Road, Great Neck, New York (516-555-5321).

During the past three years, GFI's principals have researched and developed a line of unique children's food products based on the holistic health concept—if the whole body is supplied with proper nutrition, it will, in many cases, remain healthy and free of disease.

Holism is the theory that living organisms should be viewed and treated as whole beings and not merely as the sum of different parts. The holistic concept, which *Health Food Consumer* determined is

widely accepted among adult consumers of health foods, is new to the
child-care field.

Hence, GFI plans to take advantage of the opportunities for market
development and penetration that its principals are confident exist.
GFI also believes that the existing baby-food industry pays only cursory attention to providing high-quality, nutritious products, and that
the limited number of truly healthy and nutritious baby foods creates
a market void that GFI can successfully fill.

Based on the detailed financial projections prepared by The Company's management, it is estimated that $700,000 of equity invest-
ment is required to begin the company's operations successfully. The
funds received will be used to finance initial marketing activities,
complete development of the company's product line, and provide
working capital during the first two years of operation.

Market Potential

GFI's market research shows that the United States is entering a "mini
baby boom" that will increase the potential market base for its products. This increase, combined with an expected future 25-percent annual growth rate of the $2.4 billion health food industry, as estimated
by *Health Foods Business* will increase the demand for GFI's products.
Additionally, health food products are more frequently being sold in
supermarkets, which is increasing product visibility and should help to
increase popularity.

The Company will approach the marketplace primarily through
health food stores and nature-food centers in major supermarket
chain stores, initially in the Northeast and California. Acceptance of
the GFI concept in these areas will enable the company to expand to a
national market.

The specific target markets GFI will approach through these outlets are:

Parents who are concerned about their health and their children's
    health and who thus demand higher quality and more nutri-
    tionally balanced foods and products.
Operators of child-care centers who provide meals to children.

Major Milestones

Approximately two-thirds of GFI's product line is ready to market. The remaining one-third is expected to be completed within one year.

Distinctive Competence

GFI is uniquely positioned to take advantage of this market opportunity due to the managerial and field expertise of its founders, and its products' distinct benefits.

Judith Appel, George Knapp, MD, and Samuel Knapp, MD all possess several years of experience in the child-care industry. Ms. Appel is a nutritionist and has served as director for the Children's Hospital for Special Services in White Plains, New York. In addition, she has nine years of business experience, first as marketing director for Healthy Harvest Foods in Yonkers, New York, then as owner/president of Nature's Best, Inc. Both of the Doctors Knapp have worked extensively with children in hospital-based and private practices.

Together, the principals have spent the last three years developing, refining, testing, and selling GFI's products through Nature's Best, Inc., a retail outlet in Great Neck, a Long Island suburb of New York City.

GFI's product line will satisfy the market demand for a natural, nutritious children's food. The maximum amount of nutrients will be retained in the food, providing children with more nutritional benefit than most products presently on the market. The menu items chosen will reflect the tastes most preferred by children. A broad product line will also provide a diverse meal plan.

Financial Summary

Based on detailed financial projections, if the company receives the required $700,000 in funding, it will operate profitably by year three. The following is a summary of projected financial information (dollars in thousands).

	Year 1	Year 2	Year 3	Year 4	Year 5
Sales	$1,216	$1,520	$2,653	$4,021	$5,661
Gross margin	50%	50%	50%	50%	50%
Net income after tax	$ (380)	$ (304)	$ 15	$ 404	$ 633
Net income after tax/sales	—	—	0.6%	10.0%	11.2%
Return/equity	0.0%	0.0%	10.8%	73.9%	53.6%
Return/assets	0.0%	0.0%	2.6%	44.5%	36.2%

COMMENT: EXECUTIVE SUMMARY

The company does a good job in conveying the nature of the venture on a conceptual level, then backing it up with enough detail to make the summary "stand alone" so that a potential investor who wants to make a preliminary evaluation of just the summary can do so successfully.

The cursory presentation of the principals' backgrounds is a key element of this summary. It establishes immediate credibility. Another key to the summary is the financial information, which allows one to get a sense of potential return on investment or capability of servicing debt.

The summary calls GFI a "start-up" company. It would strengthen the presentation if a more stable image could be cultivated by noting in greater detail the company's accomplishments to date. This could be done by playing more on the success the GFI line has had in its sales through Nature's Best, Inc.

A slightly more detailed major milestone summary could put the company's anticipated development into a clearer perspective. Specifically, the company should cite key benchmarks as they relate to finance, such as when profitability will be established; management, such as significant additions to the team; operations, such as the setting up of new manufacturing facilities; and marketing, such as employing new sales techniques.

6

GENERAL COMPANY DESCRIPTION

The body of the business plan begins with a general description of the company. This description should take no more than a few pages. It should present the fundamental activities and nature of the company. A fine level of detail is not appropriate in this section because the preparer will have the opportunity to offer further detail in the rest of the proposal.

This section of the plan should address questions such as: Is the company a manufacturer, retailer, or service business? What customers is it attempting to serve? What is it providing its customer base and how? Where is it located? Where will it do business (locally, nationally, internationally)?

Some further insight should also be offered as to what stage the company has reached. Is it a "seed"-stage business without a fully developed product line? Has it developed a product line, but not yet begun to market it? Or is it already marketing its products and anxious to expand its scale of activity?

It is important to articulate the business objectives. Perhaps the company is seeking a certain level of sales or geographic distribution. Or perhaps it hopes to become a publicly traded company or an attractive acquisition candidate. A statement of such objectives is important to the reviewer and may succeed in generating significant interest on the reviewer's part. Of course, these objectives must appear to be realistic and attainable.

III. GENERAL COMPANY DESCRIPTION

Good Foods, Incorporated (GFI) is a company founded on the belief that children can grow up healthier and live longer if they are fed a natural, nutritionally balanced diet starting earlier in life. GFI's goal is to increase awareness of this link between diet and health.

The GFI concept is different from traditional child-care and children's food concepts and products. It is based on the holistic approach to health, which emphasizes that if the whole body is supplied with proper nutrition, it is more likely to remain healthy and free of disease.

Accordingly, GFI has designed a diverse product line to support all the health needs of children. Furthermore, since the holistic approach not only requires proper nutrition but a program including such things as exercise, environmental stimulation, and clean water, GFI intends to deliver the entire concept through the company's supplemental educational service to parents. This will be accomplished through radio consumer education programs and consumer publications.

COMMENT: GENERAL COMPANY DESCRIPTION

The plan offers a good concise explanation of GFI. However, it makes no mention of the company's objectives. Will the company eventually go public? Will it seek to be acquired? Will it develop new lines of business? A statement of such objectives is critical to both the plan's use as a tool for future strategic planning, and, more immediately, to a reviewer's assessment of the company.

Venture investors want to know how they will eventually "get out" of an investment. They are living in a world of defined lifetimes—at least for their funds—and want investments that will be liquid within that lifetime.

7

PRODUCTS AND SERVICES

Prior to addressing in detail the business plans regarding such areas as marketing and operations, it is useful to devote attention to the business products and services. Such attention is merited on the assumption that, regardless of strategic considerations, a business cannot succeed without an appealing set of products and/or services.

Because the entrepreneur is likely to be far more familiar than the reviewer with his or her chosen field, it is important that the characteristics and the appeal of products and services be communicated in a clear and simple fashion. The following information is generally included in this section.

Physical Description. In the case of a product, a description of physical characteristics is usually appropriate. It is often helpful to include a photograph, drawing, or brochure. In the case of a service, a diagram sometimes helps to convey what is being provided by the business.

Use and Appeal. Having described the product or service in a literal sense, the entrepreneur should comment on the nature of its various uses and what constitutes its appeal. This is an opportunity to emphasize the unique features of the product or service and establish the potential of the venture.

In some instances, appeal may be based on tangible, functional benefits. For example, a certain product might accomplish a task faster or more effectively than competitive products. In other cases, appeal may depend on less tangible attributes—perhaps appearance or an aggressive marketing campaign.

Stage of Development. It is important to focus on the stage of development of the product or service, including how the company's offerings—both products and services—have evolved to their present state and how they are anticipated to evolve in the future. In particular, comments as to the offering's "readiness for market" are useful in helping the reviewer to assess the venture's viability. Detail pertaining to the research and development effort should be included as a part of the operational plan.

The objective of this part of the business plan is to convey as concisely as possible the nature of the business offerings. It is in the next section, the marketing plan, that these offerings are related to the market, and strategies and opportunities are identified. In deciding how best to present his or her offerings in the business plan to a potential investor, the entrepreneur should consider what is likely to have the greatest impact and be most easily appreciated by the reviewer. The reviewer's appreciation of a product or service can be enhanced if the entrepreneur provides insights that are not easily included in a business plan. A prototype, sample, or demonstration might be helpful.

Additionally, it is sometimes helpful to provide the reviewer with a list of experts or prior users who are familiar with the products or services and who will comment favorably on them. Such testimonials may be included in letter or report form in an appendix.

IV. PRODUCTS AND SERVICES

GFI is developing a complete line of health food products for children using minimal processing. All products contain wholesome ingredients: herbs and naturally derived vitamins, minerals, and other supplements. Products contain no chemicals or additives. Salt is never added and all foods are sweetened naturally.

Eating GFI's products in the context of the holistic dietary program the company has designed will reduce, if not eliminate, the need for supplemental vitamins.

While other companies claim to sell healthy and nutritious baby foods, their cooking processes extract many of the foods' natural nutrients. The company's unique process leaves these nutrients in the foods, resulting in a product superior in quality to those of major childrens food companies. The products have been developed over a three-year period, utilizing research data from a clinical, nutritionally oriented pediatric practice.

In addition, research information has been collected from Nature's Best, Inc. (NBI), an affiliated company that for the past three years has owned and operated a retail store selling health food products for adults and children. This store has been test marketing the childrens health food line and measuring consumer satisfaction for the past 14 months. GFI products were offered as samples for the first three months. Since then, the products have been sold successfully through NBI.

The GFI product line is designed to provide a broad range of natural food products for children. Initially, the company plans to introduce selected items, and will gradually increase the breadth of selection in each of its two major product groups. GFI plans to develop and market a complete product line of main courses, side dishes, and desserts, as it believes the market potential for these is significant. Outlined as follows are some of the key products the company plans to sell:

Child Foods

GFI has developed lines of foods for children ages 6 to 12 months and 1 to 3 years. These food products are designed to retain the maximum nutritional value of the ingredients while remaining free of artificial nutrients, chemical additives, preservatives, coloring agents, flavor enhancers, iodized salt, and refined sugar. Such additives are acknowledged by numerous industry publications, such as *Science and Health* and *The Healthy Body,* to contribute to hyperactivity in children, and are suspected to be related to dyslexia, a learning disability.

Additionally, products have been thoroughly tested for palatability, both through NBI and by an independent organization, Taste Test

Coordinators, Inc. In all tests, GFI products were at least as well received by children as Gerber's and Beech-Nut's. In some cases, children actually preferred GFI's completely natural formula to those of the well-known competitors.

In the 6- to 12-month group, traditional baby foods will be offered in four-and-one-half-ounce jars. A variety of items will be offered in the following categories: main dishes (usually a combination of meat and vegetables), meats, vegetables, desserts, fruits, and biscuits. All items will be free from artificial ingredients and will be cooked using a proprietary process that ensures they will not be robbed of their natural vitamins and minerals. A few products will be introduced initially in each category, and new products will be introduced as development funds become available and successful testing is completed.

For children ages one to three, a frozen, 100-percent-natural complete and balanced line of foods will be included in the GFI product line. These foods will be packaged in plastic bags that are to be heated in boiling water, making them convenient to prepare yet wholesome. The company will also introduce a line of sandwich meats that are prepared through a patented process and contain no chemical additives or fillers. A line of naturally sweetened snack foods specially formulated for this age group will be available in popular shapes and sizes. These items will be satisfying, yet healthy. Desserts and fruits will be the same formulations as for the 6- to 12-month group, with a greater emphasis on mixed fruits.

The following list identifies our anticipated product offerings. Most items will be available immediately; those that have an asterisk beside them will be introduced during the first year after funding.

Good Foods, Inc.
Product Listing

Six to 12 Months

Dinners:
  Chicken and mixed vegetables
  Beef and mixed vegetables
  Turkey and mixed vegetables
  *Veal and mixed vegetables
  *Beef, noodles, and vegetables
  *Macaroni, tomato, and beef

Good Foods, Inc.
Product Listing *(Continued)*

Meats:

Chicken	*Veal
Turkey	*Lamb
Beef	

Vegetables:

Peas	Mixed Vegetables
Carrots	*Spinach
Squash	*Beets
Green beans	*Sweet potatoes

Desserts:

Tapioca pudding with rice	Banana pudding
Tapioca pudding with fruit	Chocolate pudding

Fruits:

Applesauce	Mixed, in various combinations
Bananas	*Cherries
Apricots	*Peaches
Apples	*Pears

Biscuits and Cookies:

Teething biscuits	Molasses cookies

One to Three Year Olds

Prepared Foods, Main Dishes:

Spaghetti in meat sauce	*Lamb stew
*Lasagna	

Prepared Foods, Side Dishes:
    Same vegetables as in 6- to 12-month group

Sandwich Meats/Lunch Items:

Bologna	*Turkey roll
*Salami	Peanut butter

Desserts:
    Same as in 6- to 12-month group

Fruits:
    Same as in 6- to 12-month group

Biscuits and Cookies:
    Molasses cookies

The Company's Services

In addition to its health products for children, GFI plans to offer both professional and consumer education programs that will serve to promote the GFI holistic concept, increase consumer awareness of chemical additives in food and the health needs of children, and expose parents to GFI products.

George Knapp, MD and Samuel Knapp, MD, both pediatricians, have published articles on the holistic approach to children's health and will continue to do so. They have appeared and will continue to appear on radio talk shows, and they give lectures concerning holistic pediatric medicine and disease prevention. They are the major contributors to a book on pediatric medicine soon to be published, and are currently writing their own book on holistic pediatric medicine. These efforts will educate consumers and child-care professionals such as physicians, nurses, and day-care-center employees regarding the holistic approach to children's health, and expose them to GFI's products and services.

Judith Appel will offer a series of seminars to educate parents on how to improve their children's health through better nutrition. She will continue to appear on radio talk shows to discuss this subject. She is currently writing a health food cookbook and contributing regularly to a children's nutrition magazine. Ms. Appel will maintain the NBI seminar program, which instructs consumers on the importance of proper nutrition for children. She will also consult to health food store proprietors on the sale of children's health food products and the education of the retail consumer regarding child nutrition. Ms. Appel will emphasize how GFI's products, along with currently available fresh foods and health foods, can be combined to provide children with a diet that meets all of their daily nutritional needs without the addition of synthetic vitamins or minerals.

COMMENT: PRODUCTS AND SERVICES

GFI's business plan is strong here. The company outlines a broad array of products and services being offered, and yet is able to present a fairly detailed description in a concise, precise manner. The plan's authors are also able to explain the benefits of the product line in a substantive way, but one that is not overly technical. This section would be meaningful both to laypersons and experts.

8

MARKETING PLAN

The marketing section is one of the most important parts of a business plan because it communicates most directly the nature of the intended business and the manner in which that business will be able to succeed. Specifically, the purpose of the marketing section is to explain how a prospective business intends to manipulate and react to market conditions in order to generate sales.

The entrepreneur must prepare a marketing plan that is both interesting and thought-provoking. The plan cannot simply explain a concept; it must sell a prospective business as an attractive investment opportunity, a good credit risk, or a valued vendor of a product or service.

In addition, this section must be written in a manner that is meaningful to a wide variety of people, from management teams to board members, and from venture capitalists to bankers.

History has shown that the marketing challenge is one of the most critical to a company's success. Many companies with a desirable product have failed because of their marketing strategy or lack of one, and their implementation program. Therefore, reviewers give a great deal of attention to this section when evaluating a business plan. Many venture capitalists feel that some of the most important criteria for predicting the success of a new company are those factors that establish the demand for the product or service. If a real market need is not presented, all of the talent and financing in the world will not make a company successful in that product or service area.

A marketing plan may be presented in vastly different manners, depending on the type of business and the complexity of the market. The marketing techniques employed by a vendor of computer software will be considerably different from those employed by a manufacturer of heavy equipment. Similarly, the relative importance of the marketing section will depend on the prospective enterprise.

Some businesses are marketing-intensive and require a clear, compelling marketing plan. Other businesses are less marketing-intensive, and may require a less elaborate presentation. Because all businesses require sales volume to survive, however, a sound marketing program is critical and usually receives close scrutiny. Some of the most important issues that this section of the business plan should address are:

1. *Market Definition and Opportunity.* The section of the business plan that precedes the marketing section is devoted to a description of the product or service. The marketing section must establish a demand for this product or service, and should define both its market and the opportunity this market represents. Specifically, it should define the overall market, primary and secondary target-market segments, and the importance and nature of these segments.

2. *Competition and Other Influences.* Attention should be focused on market-oriented conditions that exist in the environment external to the business. Paramount among these are the degree of competition present and what impact this competition is likely to have on the enterprise. It is also important to address other forces in the external environment, such as government regulations.

3. *Marketing Strategy.* A marketing strategy must be defined. In other words, there should be some explanation as to how the business will manipulate its marketing tools. This strategy might embrace factors such as distribution, advertising and promotion, pricing, selling incentives, and location analysis. The scope and status of activities will vary depending on the

phase and potential of the company. Often, a marketing plan is phased in as the company matures. In this light, it is sometimes important to address the schedule of these activities for the period embraced by the business plan.

4. *Market Research.* Whether the market research is included as a part of the marketing plan or in a section by itself, it is often useful to present formal or informal market research, which helps to legitimize assertions. Of course, such research can also be most meaningful to the reviewer if it assists in his or her understanding of the marketplace.

5. *Sales Forecasts.* Although detailed financial projections are generally presented in the financial section of a business plan, it is often useful to present sales projections in the marketing section. This might include projected sales growth, projected market share, sales by period, sales by product or service, and sales by customer.

6. *Support Material.* It is appropriate to include in an attachment to the plan materials that might render assertions made in the plan more credible. This might include industry studies, letters of support, brochures, and reviews or articles related to the product or service.

While there is a great deal of flexibility in the creation of a marketing plan, entrepreneurs should be careful to fashion a presentation that precisely fits the characteristics of the proposed business. The key tests of a successful marketing plan are as follows:

Have a need and a market been clearly identified?

Has a clear, persuasive case been made as to how sales will be generated?

Have all relevant factors been introduced in a manner that is objective, but also in a way that will inspire confidence on the part of a reviewer?

Does this section serve as a sound basis for the implementation of a marketing strategy?

Is the section readable and interesting?

MARKET DEFINITION AND OPPORTUNITY

This part of the marketing section must establish the demand for the product or service and, therefore, the potential for the business. It is often worthwhile to begin a discussion of the market being served by presenting a general industry background. Typically, this will include a summary of industry growth or lack of growth, the sources of demand, and the way demand is satisfied.

As is often the case in the preparation of a business plan, the quality of information included in this regard is dependent on the amount of energy devoted to gathering it. Good sources for such data include trade associations, trade literature, industry studies, and industry "experts."

The degree of detail and support that should be provided may depend on the market share one requires in order to ensure success. If the market potential is commonly understood to be large and only a very small market share is projected, less detail and support information are needed. Conversely, this detailed information becomes more critical as relevant market share increases. For instance, a new steak restaurant does not need to make the claim that "Americans eat out more now than 20 years ago." It does need to point out that steakhouse-style restaurants have been doing increasingly well in its geographic area over the last two years.

After defining general market parameters, it is appropriate to identify relevant target markets, their nature, and their importance. A manufacturer of personal computers might segment its target market into three parts: in-home users, small businesses, and large corporations.

In the case of in-home users, the entrepreneur might describe the market in terms of desired product attributes, demographics, geographics, and psychographics. For instance, the in-home user may be primarily interested in a personal computer as an educational device for the family and as a means of performing home-related bookkeeping tasks. The typical purchaser might be upper-middle income or above, a homeowner, and a holder of an advanced university degree.

The plan might further specify that such individuals live in or around major metropolitan areas and that the prospective business will initially mount a marketing campaign focusing on cities with populations over 500,000 in the northeastern United States. Finally, the typical user might be described in terms of psychological characteristics. For example, this individual might be intellectual, sensitive to marketing themes based on logic (price and quality), and conservative in thought and lifestyle.

A plan would subsequently focus on all other relevant target markets in a similar manner. In addition to descriptive content, the plan should offer an evaluation of the relative attractiveness of each segment: Which markets are of primary importance? Why? Will this relative importance shift over time? Answers to such questions will be most relevant to the marketing strategy defined later in the plan.

In describing the market and associated characteristics, one must be careful to include pertinent information at an appropriate level of detail. A common mistake in business plans is to include information that is so abstract or general as to have no meaning.

V. MARKETING PLAN

Market Definition and Opportunity

GFI will direct its efforts to the sale of its products through health food retail outlets and natural food centers located within major supermarkets.

Geographically, the company will initially direct its efforts in two key areas: the Northeast, especially around New York City; and the West Coast, particularly in the Reno, Nevada and Sacramento, California area. Both of these areas have a high concentration of adult health food consumers who GFI has found, through market research and analysis, to be most receptive to health concepts for children. During the first three years of operation, the company plans to expand to three additional markets.

Company management believes their decision to include projected sales from only five markets in this plan is highly conservative. They fully anticipate increasing the number of markets during the first five years if resources are available and if such an increase would be profitable to the shareholders. To understand fully the market GFI's products will address, one must actually evaluate two separate and distinct industries:

Traditional children's food industry
Health food industry

The traditional children's food industry must be analyzed to understand the growth trends and market characteristics of the children's care industry in general. The health food industry must also be evaluated since GFI plans to market its products through retail distribution outlets currently associated primarily with the sale of adult health foods and other natural products.

Traditional Children's Food Industry

During its market research phase, GFI engaged *Vick Products Sales Research Corporation* as its marketing and advertising consulting company. Vick prepared a report on industry trends for the traditional children's food industry. In summary, the report states that

A new "mini baby boom" is on the horizon in the United States that will result in births growing at an annual rate of 2 to 5 percent at least for the first five years of the company's operations.

The per capita use of baby foods has been and is expected to continue increasing.

Two manufacturers control much of the market:

Gerber: 54 percent
Beech Nut: 17 percent
Other   29 percent

The growing number of working mothers are concerned with convenience, while all parents are more concerned with wholesomeness.

Baby food companies are introducing new products that try to fill the gap during the transition period from baby food to adult food—ages one through three years. These products have met with limited success.

Progressive Grocer magazine estimates the baby food market to account for almost $500 million in supermarket sales (excluding formula). It shows the following breakdown:

	1991 volume ($ millions)	Total (%)
Dinners	$104.45	21.7
Meats	94.32	19.6
Vegetables	66.21	13.8
Desserts	64.19	13.4
Biscuits and cookies	5.68	1.2
Cereals	49.18	10.2
Juices	81.34	16.9
All other foods	15.14	3.2
	$480.51	100.0

Due to the highly competitive nature of the traditional children's food industry, GFI has determined that the most effective way to market its products initially is through health food outlets, including single-outlet health food stores and health food chains. Natural food centers located in major supermarket chain stores will be approached as the company becomes confident of being able to service them properly. Industry experts maintain that the continued growth of health food centers in supermarket chains will greatly increase the total sales volume of all health foods. GFI plans to take advantage of this growth by aggressively selling through these outlets.

GFI's products capitalize on the trend toward wholesomeness with its unique cooking process, and on the trend toward convenience with its "boil-in" bags. Also, the company's foods for the one-to-three-year age group help fill the perceived gap between baby food and adult food, with products free from potentially harmful chemicals and additives.

Children's Health Food Industry

Since it is such a new market, industry data regarding sales of children's health food are limited. However, according to a survey in *Health Foods Business* magazine, sales of children's health foods are estimated to be .5 percent of total health food sales. In 1991, when total industry sales were estimated at $2.4 billion, children's health food sales were approximately $12 million.

GFI has obtained educated estimates from numerous health food distributors that this market will grow substantially as more companies enter it and more consumers become aware of the benefits of health-related products for children and the possible dangers of traditional children's food products.

By reviewing the history of the entire health food industry, one can begin to estimate what will occur in the children's health food industry.

From limited retail operations catering to a small group of consumers, the health food industry has grown at a 25 percent annual rate over the past 5 years as more people have come to recognize that a direct relationship exists among diet, physical exercise, and health. The medical profession, consumer groups, and government agencies have all supported this concept and the mass media have reported it widely.

Beyond this already impressive rate of sales growth for health and natural foods, these products are also becoming available in mass merchandise outlets, including both supermarkets and drug stores. As a result, expected future rate of growth for the industry should exceed the 25 percent experienced in the past. GFI, of course, will grow in conjunction with this expansion.

At present, the health food industry comprises about 8,000 retail stores, plus numerous supermarket health food sections. In 1991, an industry survey in *Natural Foods Merchandiser* magazine estimated that retail sales were approximately $2.4 billion, with $2.0 billion from individual stores and $400 million from large health food chains and supermarket health food sections.

Industry experts predict a continued high rate of growth. At present, only 9 percent of adults shop even occasionally in health food stores, and only .5 percent shop there regularly. Yet, over 35 percent of adults express a strong interest in eating more nutritional foods and in health foods specifically. Parents who hold these attitudes can also be expected to want their children to eat healthier foods.

The problem has been a lack of product exposure. This is being corrected by the rapid entry of supermarkets into the field and the development of health-food chain stores. Safemart, for example, has publicly announced that it intends to be a major health food retailer and now has "Natural Food Centers" in more than 700 of its supermarkets. One chain, Nationwide Nutrition Center, operates over 1,000 stores.

This expansion will be accompanied by a substantial increase in total volume as health food products are exposed to more retail traffic and benefit from the display and promotion of mass merchandisers.

It is still, however, important for GFI's products to gain wide acceptance in health food stores in order to establish their credibility as high-quality food items with the supermarket shoppers and distributors of health food products.

Originally, the main business of health food stores was almost exclusively vitamins, food supplements, and grains. Though these remain important categories, about 40 percent of sales are now in food products including snack foods such as cookies, potato chips, and crackers; beverages ranging from teas to soft drinks and fruit juices; and seasonings and condiments. Stores also stock a wide variety of personal care items and cosmetic products as well as some pet foods.

Health food stores are typically supplied from a combination of health food distributors and from local suppliers of perishable goods. The primary sources of supply are health food distributors, who carry some 6,000 to 8,000 items and often supply stores over a multistate area. Our research has determined that 19 distributors control between 80 and 90 percent of the retail sales volume. (For a detailed discussion, see section on distribution later in this chapter.)

Target Markets

As previously mentioned, GFI plans to approach the marketplace primarily through health food outlets and natural food centers in major supermarket chain stores. The key target markets that GFI will approach through these outlets are:

Parents who are concerned about their health and their children's health, and who demand higher quality and more nutritionally balanced foods and products

Operators of child-care centers who provide meals to children

Health Food Consumers

GFI plans to focus its initial efforts in marketing to health food consumers who have children. Approximately one-third of all households (21 million) have children under six years of age. The health food consumer will primarily purchase GFI's products at health food outlets. The characteristics of these stores were previously described.

In addition to traditional health food stores, GFI plans to direct its marketing efforts to the health food consumer through a change that is taking place in the health food industry—the entry of major supermarket chains into this market. Health food distributors with established relationships with supermarkets can be used to guarantee access to supermarket shelf space. The ability to sell its products in the natural food centers of major supermarket chains will greatly increase the exposure of the company's products to interested consumers, and hence will have a positive impact on sales.

Geographically, GFI plans to direct its initial marketing efforts toward consumers in major metropolitan areas in the Northeast and California. In the past, these areas have been the most receptive to trends in the health food industry and GFI believes initial acceptance by consumers in these areas will facilitate the acceptance of GFI products nationwide.

GFI has already established communication lines and received verbal commitments from distributors who service health food stores and natural food centers. These distributors are already familiar with NBI's product offerings and operations, as they supply most of its products.

Child-Care Centers

The increase in the number of working mothers has resulted in a corresponding rise in the number of child-care centers. It is estimated by *Parent's Choice* magazine that about 15,000 of these centers have been established throughout the country in the last 4 years alone, with an estimated 400,000 new children enrolled. These operations purchase individually or as a group, often in large volume directly from distributors. They can be made aware of GFI's products through various organizations and trade publications. The emphasis on health in child-care centers is an attraction for potential clients. This segment is expected to represent 20 percent of GFI's volume by the third year of operation.

The distributors who service institutions with other health care products will be approached to handle the distribution of GFI's products to child-care centers.

COMMENT: MARKET DEFINITION AND OPPORTUNITY

A good marketing plan should begin with a basic background of the industry and GFI is adept at presenting this. The plan offers both general thoughts and specific statistics that permit the reviewer to gain a feeling for the overall market and the way in which it is segmented. It also conveys to the reviewer that GFI is intimately familiar with the market and has expended significant effort in compiling relevant data. All of this helps to confer credibility on the plan. The

*identification of target markets in this plan is also effective. Later in
the plan, GFI identifies potential distributors by name, a detail that
could have been employed to good effect in this part of the plan as
well. Specifically, it would be helpful to cite any contracts or letters
of intent, both with potential distributors and major customers. This
helps make projected sales activity as real as possible.*

COMPETITION AND OTHER INFLUENCES

Almost without exception, the eventual performance of a prospective business will be influenced by external factors over
which the business has little or no control. Most notable is competition, although influences such as government regulation,
suppliers, and the public also need to be addressed.

In particular, attention must be focused on identifying these
influences, describing their nature and importance, and com-
menting on the likely impact of each. The following factors
must be addressed:

1. *Degree of Competition.* It is advisable to begin with some
general statement as to the level of relevant competition. The
objective in this instance is to discuss what is truly competitive
and treat it in a meaningful way.

It may be possible to identify specific businesses, products,
or services that will offer competition. In some instances, there
may be so few competitors that each is easily identifiable. Under these circumstances, it is appropriate to offer a profile of
each competitor, its relative strengths and weaknesses, and the
likely impact each will have on the start-up.

A summary of these competitive influences might be depicted in graphic or tabular form, enabling the reviewer to see
precisely how the business will stack up against its competitors.

2. *Future Sources of Competition.* While some (generally
older) industries are stable and evolve gradually, there are
many dynamic markets marked by rapid, continual change. It is

sometimes possible to anticipate such changes in the structure of the market. This attention to future competition is especially important in the case of a new product or service, where the likelihood of imitators is great; in the case of a young industry, where important changes are taking place; and in the case of a high-technology market, where state-of-the-art processes and products undergo continual evolution.

The personal computer market of the early 1980s included a proliferation of hardware manufacturers, and market share was spread thinly across many companies. As competition for retail distribution became increasingly fierce, there was a predictable shake-out in the industry. A number of companies disappeared, and market share centralized among a few. A business plan prepared for a personal computer hardware manufacturer during this period should have acknowledged the changing character of competition and explained how these market changes would affect the proposed enterprise.

3. *Other Influences.* Depending on the nature of the business, there may be other influences in the external environment worthy of being noted in a business plan.

A medical products business might be prone to rigorous Food and Drug Administration review. This process might have an impact on the speed with which new products could be introduced, their design, and the manner in which they could be marketed.

The tourism industry, as Americans saw dramatically in 1986, is susceptible to the actions of terrorists. Both terrorism in Europe and the United States' response to it hurt the foreign travel industry, helped the U.S. tourist industry, and had little effect on the airline industry. During the Gulf War in 1991, the threat of more terrorism drove the tourism and travel industry into a tailspin that sent airlines, travel agents, hotels and other industry segments scrambling.

The important point to recognize is that there may be significant external influences other than competition that have an impact on how new products are sold. Such influences should

be treated in the marketing section of a business plan in a manner similar to the way competition is treated.

COMPETITION AND OTHER INFLUENCES

GFI can expect to face competition from two key areas: first, traditional children's food suppliers, and second, the health food trade. A
discussion of each is presented as follows:

Traditional Children's Food Industry

As mentioned previously, the children's food industry is highly competitive, with a small number of very powerful suppliers. Two children's food manufacturers currently supply 71 percent of the industry.

The largest of these companies operates with an advertising budget
in excess of $20 million. In view of these companies' market domi-
nance, GFI has developed an initial approach to marketing that will
focus on outlets other than mass merchandisers. However, there is a
development in the mass-merchandiser/traditional children's food
market that is of importance to GFI's activities.

As with mass-market food products for adults, there has been a no-
ticeable trend towards food products for children that make nutritional or quasi-nutritional claims. This trend is helpful to GFI in that it
increases consumer awareness of the importance of nutrition. However, these products are not competing with those of GFI because they
are primarily sold in the children's-food sections of standard supermarkets. GFI believes the nutritional value and quality of these traditional manufacturers' items will be viewed as inferior as consumers
become aware of health-food products.

Health Food Trade

More direct competition is to be found in the health food trade. Competition here is of three forms: broad-line companies who market
some child-related products; those who sell a few selected children's

items such as cereals; and local companies who supply children's foods in a limited geographical area.

Selected companies in this latter category are beginning to expand their product lines and appear to be planning for national distribution. GFI believes it is well equipped to compete in this market, because of its extensive market and product research to date, the expertise of its principals, the retail knowledge gained through the NBI store, and its already well-developed product line.

Although NBI is a single retail shop, GFI will also gain mass market expertise from its sales staff and distributors. The company initially plans to focus on two major geographical markets—the Northeast and California. Acceptance of the GFI concept in these areas will position the company for expansion into the national market as funds become available.

Competitive Analysis

It can be expected that some competitors will react to GFI's entrance into this market. The traditional children's-food industry participants have already reacted to what they perceive as changes in the marketplace. They have altered their marketing approach to emphasize that their products are natural, with no artificial additives or sweeteners.

Because of this, and the fact that GFI will not display its products alongside the traditional products (only in the health food sections of supermarkets and in health food stores) GFI expects moderate adverse reaction by these companies to its introduction. GFI's advertising and promotion campaign will clearly differentiate its "holistic" products from those of its competitors.

GFI expects the most direct competition to come from other manufacturers of health foods, who will eventually recognize the potential market for children's health foods. GFI's large head start in the development and test marketing of these products will give it an advantage that will be difficult for later entrants to overcome.

Included in Attachment B is a summary of the companies GFI considers its major competitors and some important characteristics of each.

GFI's Competitive Edge

GFI will be the only company in the industry that markets a complete health food product line for children and a comprehensive education program aimed at increasing awareness of the holistic concept, thereby increasing sales of its products.

The company's entire marketing effort will be in the area of health food for children, and the company's product sales will benefit from the broad-based appeal generated through the numerous retail outlets GFI plans to utilize. This focus will distinguish GFI from competing health food companies such as Familia and Health Valley. These companies offer a broad line of adult-oriented products to which they have added a narrow line of children's products. GFI will distinguish itself from the major baby food makers by positioning itself as a maker of superior quality health-food products.

Price Competition

GFI intends to position its products as slightly higher priced health care items, due to its complete line and services. It is estimated that this will place GFI products 15 to 18 percent above the suggested retail price of the products of the major baby food producers.

COMMENT: COMPETITION AND OTHER INFLUENCES

In this section of the plan GFI addresses a number of issues:

It identifies competition in the marketplace in a general way.

By reference to an attachment, it specifically identifies competitive companies along with their relevant characteristics.

It anticipates the impact of competition on its own performance.

It explains its competitive advantages.

These issues are all appropriate and should be addressed in most business plans.

If this section has a shortcoming, it is that it appears to dismiss competition too lightly. No real threats are acknowledged, which perhaps is an objective assessment but more than likely is overly optimistic. Only in the last paragraph is mention made of price differences between GFI and competition, and the reader must take it on faith that even if the target market is as big as GFI believes it to be, people will be willing to pay such a high premium.

In order to be complete, GFI should note influences other than competition that will have an impact on their marketing activity. Most notably missing is the impact of FDA regulations as they pertain to marketing. This is briefly addressed in the operations section, but should be addressed here also.

MARKETING STRATEGY

Having defined the relevant market and its opportunities, one must address how the prospective business will exploit these opportunities. A marketing strategy that explains how the business will organize and implement its marketing plans in order to achieve desired sales performance must be presented. This involves focusing attention on each salient marketing tool a company has at its disposal.

Elements such as distribution, pricing strategy, advertising, promotion, site analysis, and related budgets all may merit discussion, depending on their importance in relation to the company's overall market strategy. While meticulous detail is probably unnecessary, it is important that the reviewer gain a general understanding of how the business intends to actively market its product or service.

Some of the marketing variables commonly addressed in the business plan are:

1. *Sales and Distribution Strategy.* One possible place to begin a discussion of marketing strategy is with the mechanisms and vehicles a business will use to get its products or services to customers. Will the business employ its own sales force for

direct marketing or will dealers, distributors, or jobbers be used? Have any of these distribution people been specifically identified? On what basis will they be or have they been selected? How will they be compensated? What incentives will be offered?

In some instances, the organization of a selling and distribution network is relatively uncomplicated, with only basic descriptions required. In other instances, a more detailed presentation will be appropriate.

In a case where the business will rely on its own sales force, it might be important to communicate whether the salespeople will require special skills. For instance, a technical product might require a sales force with the appropriate technical background.

Specific selling procedures that will be employed, such as "cold calls" or formal presentations, may merit attention. The number of salespeople and the manner in which they will be assigned—by product or geographic territory—may also be worthy of description. Finally, a commission or other incentive program might be described.

2. *Pricing Strategy.* There is a good likelihood that pricing will be an important element in the overall market strategy. While an actual price list is not critical, the general pricing structure and the rationale behind this structure should be provided. Policy regarding discounting and price changes should be addressed as well as the impact of pricing strategy as a whole on gross profit (revenue less cost of goods sold).

For example, the manufacturer of designer women's apparel may pursue a high-price strategy, then discount liberally as a means of generating sales. He may adjust prices in response to changes in the cost of labor and material, as well as what part of the season he is in. The result might be a gross profit somewhat higher than industry norms.

If a detailed price list has been developed and is important to the reviewer's understanding, it may be summarized or included as an attachment.

3. *Advertising, Public Relations, and Promotion.* In many instances, advertising, public relations, and promotion will play an important role in the company's attempts to generate sales. The business's intentions in this regard should be conveyed in concise, basic terms. One way of accomplishing this is to focus on the concept and creative content of the communications campaign, the vehicles that will be utilized, such as electronic media, print media, or direct mail, and the extent to which each will be employed. If the services of a professional agency will be used, a statement about that is appropriate.

Many start-up or early-stage companies will not have a large advertising budget, if they have any advertising budget at all. For them, public relations is often within reach. Although public relations campaigns mounted by large, well-known agencies can be more expensive than advertising campaigns, public relations can be done on an adhoc basis and on a shoestring budget. Entrepreneurs can contact local media—newspapers, radio, and television—which often write or broadcast stories on new businesses in the community.

Newspaper articles that are generated this way can reach a wide audience and may serve as "free advertising," to the extent that the newspaper says something nice about the business or product. Newspaper clippings also convey a sense of objectivity, which can help project an image without being self-serving.

It may be unwise to describe this communication strategy too explicitly, especially if this is a relatively new venture. Advertising and promotion strategy often changes as companies develop (although the description of the advertising and promotional program may present an excellent opportunity to sell the company's potential).

4. *Site Analysis.* In some instances, particularly if the business will engage in retail activity, discussion of location is critical to assessing the effectiveness of a marketing strategy. There are a number of key variables that might be addressed in this regard, including demographics of the surrounding population,

accessibility, visibility, and cost. These may be addressed conceptually, or if a site or sites have already been chosen, an actual profile might be included. If the physical nature of the facility is important, a specific description might also be worthwhile. An artist's rendering, plot plan, or map often enhances the reviewer's understanding. These items might best be included in an attachment.

5. *Related Budgets.* The entrepreneur may wish to offer a basic marketing budget. Although detailed financial information will be included in the plan's financial section, some budget information may be useful here.

Pie charts, graphs, tables, and other graphics can be most effective in presenting precisely how the overall marketing effort will be organized and how the business's resources will be allocated among various marketing tools. These might also help the reviewer understand the relative importance of each component of the strategy.

6. *Future Marketing Activities.* While other sections of the plan will focus attention on the company's future products and growth, the marketing plan, when appropriate, should discuss sales strategies contemplated to perpetuate growth.

For example, a company's immediate plans might involve penetrating only the domestic market, while in the future the same company might consider a license for its products in some international markets, or perhaps even a joint venture. A manufacturer might employ limited promotion and advertising in the near term due to modest financial resources. However, more extensive advertising might be contemplated at a later date after greater financial resources have been secured.

In each of these scenarios, the ultimate development of a business depends significantly on strategies employed in the medium to long term. These kinds of plans should be presented, though it may be necessary to relate them in a vague manner. The timing of the strategy and the strategy itself will probably be affected by intervening events. In general, less detail should be offered as the business plan addresses itself to activities to be undertaken further in the future.

MARKETING STRATEGY

Initially, the company plans to limit its sales efforts to the following areas:

Through health food distributors to health food stores

Through health food distributors and other specialty food distributors to supermarkets and other mass merchandisers active in health food retailing

By aggressively merchandising a comprehensive line that meets the highest health and nutritional standards, GFI plans to dominate the chosen distribution channels.

Advertising, Public Relations, and Promotion

The specific details of the marketing programs and strategies will be developed by the company's marketing and advertising consulting firm, *Vick Products Sales Research Corporation,* during the first three months of the company's operations. This summary outlines the market programs and specific implementation strategies planned:

1. *Public Relations.* GFI's principals plan to continue the public relations efforts in which they are currently involved, such as appearing on radio talk shows and with local interest groups and writing articles and books. These efforts will be formalized further so that the GFI story can be appropriately developed and positioned in the media to generate significant ongoing coverage.

The programs will incorporate the uniqueness of the concept, the prevention and health-promoting qualities of the products, and the experience of the technical and professional staff. The objective will be to increase awareness of the relationship between diet and health.

2. *Advertising.* **Materials will be developed that promote the uniqueness and quality of GFI products. Although the specific types of media to be utilized and the level of activity have not yet been completely defined, GFI expects that the majority of its advertising will take the form of print advertisements in industry publications. These publications, for each consumer group, include:**

> **Retail Health Food Industry. Eight major magazines for the consumer:** *Let's Live, Prevention, Whole Life Times, Bestways, Chimo, East-West Journal, Health Quarterly Plus 2,* **and** *Vegetarian Times.*

> **Industrial Health Food Industry. Four major trade journals for industry distributors, jobbers, and retailers:** *Natural Foods Merchandiser, Natural Foods Business, Health Foods Retailing,* **and** *Whole Foods.*

> **Family/Parenting. There are nine magazines:** *American Family, Bulletin of Maternal and Child Health, Family, Mothering, Parents, Parent's Choice, Practical Parenting, Redbook's Young Mother,* **and** *The Single Parent.*

The program will be designed to use the specific advertising media that will generate the most exposure for The Company and its products.

3. *Sales Promotion.* **Appropriate incentive programs will be developed that will gain and keep the attention of the trade as well as the consumer.**

4. *Packaging and Point-of-Sale Material.* **Packaging that promotes the message of health and superior quality will be developed. It will be designed to educate the consumer about the holistic concept, to create consumer awareness of the point of sale and clearly define the specific products in GFI's line. Materials will be created, designed, and executed for use in retail outlets and will include shelf talkers, posters, and display units. In addition, the company plans to offer literature about the products and the holistic approach to child health.**

Distribution

GFI has thoroughly investigated and is familiar with the distribution route of both the health food and children's food industries. A summary of the existing distribution channels is provided as follows.

Health food stores, co-ops, and health food chains are supplied through traditional health food distributors. Natural food sections of supermarkets are supplied either in the same way or by food brokers who deal in specialty, gourmet, or health foods. Child-care centers are supplied directly by distributors.

The health food industry is very efficient at the wholesale level, as just 19 distributors give a manufacturer access to 80 to 90 percent of retail sales volume.

The key distributors, their locations, and ownership affiliations, are:

Distributor	Location	Group
Northwest Health Food[a]	Seattle	Well-Balanced Foods
Weisberg Foods[a]	Portland, OR	Independent
Porter Distribution[a]	San Francisco	Friendly Foods
Serlen & Sivin[a]	Los Angeles	Independent
Nature's Best[a]	Los Angeles	Independent
Foods for Health	Phoenix	Independent
Edelstein Distributors[a]	Dallas	Friendly Foods
Roberts Southwest[a]	Tulsa	Well-Balanced Foods
Colorado Foods	Denver	Independent
Savory Foods	Minneapolis	Independent
Health Foods, Inc.	Chicago	Independent
Central U.S. Nat. Foods	Ann Arbor	Well-Balanced Foods
Nash Foods	Boston	Independent
Well-Balanced Foods[a]	New York	Well-Balanced Foods
Hecht Distributors[a]	New York	Friendly Foods
Lynch Foods[a]	New York	Independent
Savage Foods	Tennessee	Friendly Foods
MCG Distributors[a]	Florida	Well-Balanced Foods
Stein's Food Emporium	Florida	Eat-Rite

[a]Aware of GFI's products.

COMMENT: MARKETING STRATEGY

GFI begins this section by defining a "niche" strategy, which hinges on selling through health food distributors. This focus on a niche is often an effective approach for a new company, especially one with limited resources. By focusing resources narrowly, the company is more likely to achieve its desired result.

The company's attention to advertising and distribution is thorough and pragmatic. Plans for continued public relations are likely to be especially effective. The company should expect the prospective investor or leader to contact some of the distributors listed to gauge their reaction to the GFI product line. This is a natural part of the "due diligence" process.

To the extent that GFI can introduce through the plan objective parties who will comment favorably on the product line, they will establish great credibility.

As we see later in the plan, GFI has done more than simply list distributors. The company has initiated conversations and cultivated interest.

MARKET RESEARCH

The purpose of including some market research in the business plan is to enhance the entrepreneur's and reviewers' understanding of the market, as well as to enhance the plan's credibility to the reviewer.

In addition, preliminary market research included in the business plan can help one formulate marketing strategy and can be a first step in selling by facilitating contact with respondents who had positive reactions to the product or service.

A quick cost/benefit analysis must be done to see what kind of preliminary research will be most effective. Research for a business plan does not need to be elaborate. Remember the reason the research is being conducted—for a first cut at information, not necessarily for statistically valid samples or other elegant research techniques. In some markets, secondary research—in the form of a literature search—may be as good as primary research.

One owner of a bookstore used to conduct market research by going into a major bookstore-chain store just before lunch time, counting the number of copies of some major titles, then going into the same store a few hours later after the rush to see which titles were sold. That was how he knew how to stock his own shelves. A few years later he sold his business—a chain of 17 bookstores—for a healthy profit.

Entrepreneurs should not get hung up on their limited funds to do market research. Most companies that write business plans with the intention of submitting them for review by potential investors are in the same boat.

Since the mid 1980s, information technology has put more and more powerful market research tools at the disposal of businesses with the most modest budgets. There are databases of material one would need to analyze virtually any market, and software to download the databases at high speed, then analyze the material using a personal or laptop computer.

Increasingly, databases are available on CD-ROM optical disc technology in libraries, eliminating the cost of downloading via telephone lines. With a good business library at your disposal and a little assistance from a competent reference librarian who has a thorough knowledge of what various databases are and the easiest/least expensive way to access them, you can create sophisticated market research.

The downside of all this is that as more and more proposers put together market research of this caliber, reviewers' expectations are increased, and this level will become a normal effort for all proposers when developing a business plan.

MARKET RESEARCH

The Nature's Best, Incorporated® Store.
Three years ago the NBI retail health food store for children was opened in Great Neck, New York.

The store was established as a result of Judith Appel's desire to prove that better nutrition for children provided a viable commercial opportunity. The GFI products have been sold to NBI's customers with very favorable results. Great Neck is regarded as representative of the average middle- to upper-income consumer population. This is GFI's target market, since this population is most aware of current social issues. The company believes the success of the NBI operation demonstrates the general viability of its concept.

Other Market Research

Significant market research and analysis was undertaken prior to the preparation of this marketing plan.

Two major studies of the health food industry have been purchased:

1. *Mass Merchandised Health Foods: Market Trends,* **published by Business Communications International (1990)**
2. *The Health and Natural Food Market,* **published by Business Trend Analysts, Inc. (1991)**

George Knapp and Judith Appel have traveled extensively throughout the United States, including several trips to the West Coast, to develop an understanding of the retail and wholesale health food market. In addition, they have attended the national health food and products conventions and all regional shows. They provided an education booth explaining the company's products and concepts at some of these shows, and have been able to determine that significant interest exists on the part of retailers.

They have visited distributors in both the children's products and health food industries. During these numerous visits they have developed an excellent understanding of the distribution channels of both industries, which they have incorporated into this plan.

Reaction from Distributors and Retailers

The GFI concept and proposed product line has been exposed on a confidential basis to a small number of key distributors and retailers.

These accounts represent a significant percentage of industry sales and would be crucial to success. Summaries of the responses are outlined as follows:

Susie's Produce Market, Sacramento, California

Susie's, with 36 stores, is the leading supermarket retailer of health foods in the country. Company representatives stated that they would place the full line in all stores as soon as it is available. Furthermore, they expressed a strong desire to have the opportunity to be the first chain to introduce the line.

Safemart Stores, Northern California Division

This 196-store group is the leading division within the Safemart chain, with over 70 natural food center installations. A company representative stated that the company would approve the line for all sufficiently large centers.

Serlen & Sivin, Los Angeles, California

S & S is the largest health food distributor on the West Coast and accounts for as much as 7 to 10 percent of national volume. In addition to supplying health food stores, S & S supplies about 600 supermarkets, mainly through its Quality Brands division.

This distributor considers children's products a grossly underdeveloped category in the health food industry. No one is effectively merchandising a full line; yet such a line is consistent with the desires of larger stores to serve more of their customers' needs. S & S representatives maintained they would purchase and support the full line.

Roberts Southwest Distributors, Tulsa, Oklahoma

Roberts is the largest distributor in the West, serving about 1,500 stores plus four Safemart divisions. The company sees opportunities in this market and would expect to purchase the line.

Well-Balanced Foods, Ridgefield, New Jersey

Well-Balanced Foods is the leading distributor in the East and is the parent company of four other distributors. This very selective distributor has said that, due to GFI's credentials and the completeness of the line, it would be very interested in distributing the company's products.

Lynch Foods, Bronx, New York
Representatives from this well-respected distributor have stated that, due to the completeness of the line and the professional credentials of GFI's principals, it would be very interested in distributing the company's products.

COMMENT: MARKET RESEARCH

This part of the plan is an excellent example of how a company can most effectively employ a low budget, "seat-of-the-pants" approach to market research.

While many people think of market research in terms of statistically valid samples, test markets, and focus groups, GFI's approach is simply to contact key decision makers in both distribution and retail and seek their comments and approval. The company bases these insights on a base of knowledge gained from the purchase of existing market studies.

In addition to providing important, practical knowledge (as opposed to an abstract study), this research represents the first step in actively marketing a product.

Sometimes, it is most effective for entrepreneurs to approach customers and say, in effect, "Tell me what you want me to be. How will I be most appealing?" This represents the extreme of being "market driven."

During the later part of his first term in office nearly 10 years ago, New York mayor Edward Koch would walk the streets of the city for a couple of hours every day, stopping people, shaking their hands, and saying: "Hi, I'm Ed Koch, how am I doing?" Today, with instant polling, politicians are barraged with public opinion about how they are doing. Perhaps politicians are the supreme example of a product being market driven.

SALES FORECASTS

Though projected financial performance is presented in detail in the plan's financial section, a sales analysis included in this section can be an effective means of explaining and justifying anticipated sales volume. This analysis may be presented in a number of formats, so long as it enhances the credibility of forecasted performance. Some kinds of analysis are:

1. *Sales by Period.* It is most useful to present sales as a function of time, in order to demonstrate anticipated growth and patterns such as seasonability. This has important ramifications with regard to cash flow and anticipated capital requirements. Such performance may be depicted in graphic or tabular form, though some narrative should be included explaining the rationale for the analysis.

It is often valuable to present multiple sales forecasts. Typically, conservative, "most-likely," and optimistic forecasts are given. These projections must all be reasonable, or the validity of the entire presentation may be questioned.

These forecasts are especially important in the development of financial plans, since a more optimistic and aggressive plan often requires more cash and usually results in higher profits. Remember, sophisticated investors evaluate the company and their investment based on their belief in the company's growth potential and market value.

2. *Sales by Products or Services.* A breakdown of sales by product or service may be presented if more than one product or service is being offered. This breakdown is useful in communicating the relative importance of each of the business's products. It can also serve to explain the company's priorities and the manner in which it will allocate resources. If the business has a great number of products, it may be helpful to group these into general categories such as retail sales, service, and consulting. Again, conveying the data graphically is useful.

3. *Sales by Customer Group.* It may be helpful to categorize projected sales by customer group.

For example, an independent pathology laboratory might anticipate that 50 percent of sales volume will come from hospitals on a contract basis, 25 percent from group practices and medical associations, and 25 percent from independent physicians.

If the entrepreneur can go one step further and document these sources with contracts or letters of intent, projected sales volume will become far more credible to the reviewer.

4. *Market Share.* One conventional means of measuring sales performance is market share; that is, the percentage of the total market sales the proposed company expects to capture.

For example, if the market sales in a particular instance are $100 million and the business projects $10 million in sales, the anticipated market share is 10 percent.

In itself, this statistic has little meaning. After carefully defining the relevant market and the level of competition, however, this measure becomes far more significant. It should be noted that market share might not have any meaning in the case where market size dwarfs the significance of any single company.

Note that GFI includes a number of relevant sales forecasts in an attachment at the end of its plan.

SUPPORT MATERIAL

Though there is a danger in presenting too much information in the marketing section of a business plan, there is clearly a need to include enough detail to make the presentation as compelling as possible. If there is doubt as to whether certain information is excessive, it is best to include that material in an attachment.

This is especially appropriate in the case of legitimizing or supporting documentation, such as letters of intent, letters of support, flattering articles and reviews, brochures, artists' renderings, and industry studies. While this material is not central to communicating a concept, it is useful in making the business plan a more effective sales document.

9

OPERATIONAL PLAN

One set of fundamental issues a business plan must address is how the business will create its products and services. Questions this part of the plan must answer include:

What is the general approach to manufacturing?

What are the sources of raw materials?

What processes will be used in manufacturing?

What are the labor requirements?

How will suppliers and vendors be used?

Because the business plan has the objectives of both planning and raising capital, the entrepreneur may have some difficulty striking the proper balance between sophistication and simplicity in explaining the sometimes complicated manufacturing and process technologies.

As an internal planning document, the plan should be a detailed, in-depth operational plan. This will give the entrepreneur an opportunity to work out many potential problems on paper prior to commencing operations. As a sales tool to be reviewed by external parties, however, the content of the operational plan may have to be more straightforward.

In some cases, the business's operations may constitute an important part of its appeal. This argues for a relatively detailed presentation. Yet an overly technical and complicated presentation might make review of the plan difficult and, as a result, be counterproductive. One should weigh what will be meaningful to reviewers in terms of two questions:

1. Will the reviewer understand the content?
2. How important is the content to the overall understanding and appreciation of the business plan?

The relative importance of an operational plan will depend on the nature of the business. A production facility will probably require significant attention to operational issues. In contrast, most retail businesses and some service businesses will probably have less operational complexity.

Some issues often addressed in an operational plan include:

1. *Product Development.* It is not unusual to prepare a business plan before a business's full range of products and services is developed. This is especially true of a start-up company. Even after goods have been developed, it is often necessary for a company to continue its development effort in order to maintain its competitive position and promote a healthy, evolutionary process. In this light, it is worthwhile to present a summary of the development activities that the company will undertake.

2. *Manufacturing.* In the case of a production facility, it is important to discuss the process by which a company will manufacture its products. This usually involves some description of the plant, equipment, material, and labor requirements; the techniques and processes that will be employed in combining these resources, such as assembly lines and robotics; and the capability of the business in terms of production rates, critical constraints such as productive capacity, or quality assurance programs.

3. *Maintenance and Service.* In some instances, it is important for a company to define the service and support it will provide. Specifically, the plan should address the level of support a company will provide after a customer has purchased a product or

service. This is particularly important in the case of a new or technical product.

4. *External Influences.* In some instances there are external influences worth discussing, such as pollution control regulations or Occupational Safety and Health Administration (OSHA) requirements. This part of the operational plan affords the entrepreneur an opportunity to address factors out of his or her control that have an impact on the manner of operation. Flow charts, diagrams, and charts are effective in presenting this type of information.

PRODUCT DEVELOPMENT

A business plan can be prepared at any stage in a company's life. It might focus on a rank start-up, perhaps even a company that has not yet developed its array of products and services. Similarly, it might present an infant-stage company with only a brief operating history. At the other extreme, a business plan might picture a mature or declining company that must evolve further if it is to maintain a vigorous presence in the marketplace.

In any of these instances, it is important to communicate development efforts designed to further the company's products. This clearly is critical to a manufacturer of high-tech products who must remain "state-of-the-art." Even a company that manufactures "low-tech" products might employ high-tech or evolving processes. The development effort in this case would focus on the manufacturing process rather than the end product. For example, a printing company might continue to produce the same product, but the use of advanced, computer-based typesetting equipment might enhance product quality and productivity.

Retail and service companies may also place a high priority on developing operations to enhance performance. A department store might develop surveillance systems to help reduce "shrinkage" from shoplifting or employee theft. Even efforts to develop more attractive, enjoyable shopping environments might be included in a business plan in a section devoted to product development.

Attention to product development is not always warranted in a business plan. In many instances, such effort may be unimportant to the company's activities.

The replication of a single retail outlet into a chain of stores, for example, may involve little or no product development. Changes in the concept might be subtle and unplanned, with no formal effort being channeled into development activity.

There are several practical points one should bear in mind when addressing product development:

1. Perhaps most importantly, the gap between an idea or design and an actual product—or at least a functioning prototype—is a critical gap. If such a gap exists, the plan must demonstrate as explicitly as possible how it will be bridged.

Lenders are typically reluctant to finance a business whose products are still on paper. Venture capitalists have begun to show some flexibility in this regard, but they often exhibit a similar reluctance. Such a reluctance may prove to be a formidable obstacle in the launching of a venture.

2. The product development section can easily slip into being a scientific or research treatise. Exploiting such an opportunity is a mistake. The entrepreneur should present development activity in basic terms. More detailed, technical material can be submitted as supplemental information if appropriate. In such an instance, a reference to the availability of such information should be included in this part of the plan.

3. It is often more compelling to present in detail the technical team rather than the research itself. The capabilities and past accomplishments of the team members are likely to be more easily understood and appreciated by the reviewer.

VI. OPERATIONAL PLAN

Product Development

Much of the time and effort during GFI's first three years has been spent on research and product development.

Current Product Development Status

A previous list (see Chapter 7) showed the products GFI has developed. Most of these products are currently ready to market and will be the focus of the company's initial marketing efforts.

Each of these products has been tested for palatability, nutrition, and health through a variety of means, including:

Distribution to users through the NBI stores

Distribution through the pediatric practice with which Drs. Knapp are associated

Independent palatability tests conducted by Taste Test Coordinators, Inc.

The product formulations have been changed and refined to produce the best possible results. Final tests were successful with regard to all of the evaluation criteria established. Results of these tests are available on request.

Several other products require a limited amount of developmental work in the first year of GFI's operations. For these products, final formulation adjustment and fine tuning are required, as well as final testing for palatability. They are expected to be ready for market by the middle of the company's second year in operation.

In addition to the products listed in the first list, GFI is researching certain additional products. These include vitamin and mineral formulations, an expanded line of frozen prepared foods, and snacks. GFI management plans to conduct development of these products when the company's other products are generating sufficient cash to provide the funds required.

COMMENT: PRODUCT DEVELOPMENT

GFI's plan is brief here, and appropriately so. It seems to cover most of the key points, with one notable exception: The company does not explain the extent to which its product line is proprietary and the ability (or lack of same) of others to imitate it.

When preparing this part of the plan, the entrepreneur should relate what impact development activity has on competition, and vice versa.

MANUFACTURING

Integral to the overall understanding of a production-oriented business is an appreciation of how the company will manufacture its products. One straightforward way of conveying such information is to examine this activity in terms of resources, processes, and output.

Resources may be characterized as those elements the firm must utilize in an effort to manufacture a desired product. Typically, these include manufacturing facilities, machinery, equipment, materials and related assets, and labor. Depending on their relative importance, attention might be focused on each of these elements.

Since start-up or expansion capital is often used for the acquisition of tangible assets, it is usually appropriate to comment on the sources of these assets, their nature, and the role they will play in the production effort.

This discussion might include a profile of the facility that will be used, including comments regarding size, location, and related specifications—clearance, loading docks, and proximity to rail outlets and airports. There should be some comment as to the nature of the machinery and equipment being acquired, its capabilities and constraints, and the anticipated vendor(s). Also, sources of raw materials or components, availability, price volatility, and key supplier relationships are often worth mentioning.

A discussion of labor requirements is central to a complete understanding of a business's operational nature. Rather than detailing the precise responsibilities of each employee, general background, and special requirements should be given.

In some cases it is helpful to present an organizational chart that depicts the business's structure in terms of reporting responsibilities and interrelationships. Such a chart communicates not only how human resources will be allocated, but how work, in general, will be done. These factors can also be addressed in a section devoted exclusively to personnel and organization.

After describing the production elements, it is important to discuss the production processes that will be used. An illustration or flow chart can show this effectively. Some companies operate on an assembly-line basis, for instance, while others organize as a job shop.

In addition, it is helpful to mention the resource mix. Some companies elect a labor-intensive route while others depend heavily on automation.

Finally, some comment should be made about what processes will be done in-house and what work will be contracted out. One way many start-up and infant companies reduce initial capital requirements is by contracting many functions out.

There should be some description of the manufacturing output. Although there is ample opportunity in other parts of the business plan to discuss the nature and appeal of various goods, it is important to discuss related issues in the operational plan. For example, it might be important to examine plant capacity or other limiting factors. In the short term, this capacity may represent a cap on potential financial performance.

In addition to quantity of output, it is helpful to comment on quality-control plans and anticipated defect rates.

Practical points related to the manufacturing process include the following:

1. Investors, and especially lenders, are anxious to see that entrepreneurs have accurately projected their capital

requirements and indicated the sources of funding for these acquisitions if not from the funds being sought. Clearly, it would be most undesirable for a company to exhaust its financial resources before addressing all of its needs.

The plan preparer must use judgment in deciding how much detail should be offered in this regard. At one extreme, certain lenders might request a precise breakdown of asset requirements documented by quotations from suppliers. In many other instances, more aggregated data with little or no documentation may be appropriate. The entrepreneur must be sensitive to the desires of the reviewer in deciding what material to include.

2. In preparing an operational plan, it is often important to consider the impact of growth on operations. Will plant size have to increase in the near term? Will more machinery and equipment be required? And, most importantly, will further rounds of financing be required as a result?

3. While a section devoted to manufacturing is appropriate in the instance of a manufacturing company, a description analogous to this is often warranted in the case of a service or retail business. In these instances, there will be a change in presentation, but it is still important that some insight be offered on how the business will operate in terms of key supplier relationships, division of responsibilities, and other areas. For example, a retail business will have to describe the resources and processes necessary to move inventory, maintain security, and serve the clientele.

MANUFACTURING

Processing Techniques

Unlike traditional children's food manufacturers, GFI uses the "least processing method," for food production. The less the food is processed, cooked, steamed, extruded, and mixed with chemicals, the more health supporting factors will remain.

Planned Operations

GFI plans to subcontract the production of its products to outsiders. Accordingly, the company has contacted other food-processing companies and has entered into a verbal agreement to manufacture with one such company.

The company satisfactorily produced test batches in the spring of 1984. These batches were given away at the NBI store as part of a controlled research project conducted by GFI.

GFI will not make its complete product formulations available to outsiders. Accordingly, the company will provide premix (a special mixture of key ingredients) to the subcontractors. GFI will produce the premix for all products in its Westchester County, New York, plant through the first two years of operations.

The director of research and development will oversee the premix manufacturing and quality testing. Three employees will be responsible for producing the premix. This number will increase with the growth in sales.

As demand increases, GFI will establish a premix facility on the West Coast and contract with a West Coast food-processing company to supply the Western markets. As a result, the company will maintain control of the key ingredients of its product formulations. Those premix facilities will also have the responsibility for product quality testing.

Subcontractors will package the product. GFI will be introducing a unique packaging concept for baby food: the four pack. Instead of buying several loose jars, the consumer will be offered the convenience of a proven and well-accepted packaging method. The subcontractor will package four identical products or a mix of four varieties within each product group.

In its verbal agreement, the food processor has offered to maintain all inventory and to ship directly to distributors. The subcontractor has sufficient capacity to handle the growth expected within the two initial markets. When the third market is entered, in year three, a second subcontractor will be hired on the West Coast. GFI, therefore, does not anticipate any problems with satisfying the order volume.

Production Costs

Through its own research and discussions with contractors, GFI has estimated its cost of sales. GFI obtained verbal price quotes from a number of manufacturers in order to determine production costs. The subcontractors will be responsible for controlling raw material and labor costs, excluding the premix. Their estimates have been incorporated into the cost projections included in the attached financial projections.

Facilities and Properties

The company expects to operate from rented facilities on Pearl Street in Yonkers, New York, and at 271 Prospect Lane in Great Neck, New York.

At the Prospect Lane location, GFI will continue to maintain a 2,700-square-foot office on the second floor above the NBI health food store.

The plant in Yonkers will be the premix facility referred to previously. Administrative activities will occupy 800 square feet of the 3,000-square-foot facility. As GFI expands geographically, a second premix facility will begin operations on the West Coast. In year three the company expects to relocate marketing, research, and administration activities to facilities of approximately 5,000 square feet.

COMMENT: MANUFACTURING

To the extent that GFI subcontracts manufacturing activity, it simplifies this part of the business plan. From a practical point of view, it means there will be somewhat less complexity in starting the company and a reduced capital requirement.

GFI also addresses the question of manufacturing in the future assuming increased sales volume. Specifically, it addresses the question of production constraints, which is important. If the company hopes for rapid growth in sales, it had better have the production capacity to satisfy this growth.

The company slightly glosses over the manufacturing of premix. It would be interesting to note prospective problems and issues such as shelf life and the necessity for special clean manufacturing facilities.

SERVICE AND SUPPORT

The service and support of a company's goods are often critical to the business's success. As a consequence, they often merit attention in the business plan. The appropriateness of such description is dependent on the nature of the company's products. Some goods are sufficiently simple or inexpensive not to need service and support. In other instances, such as technical or new products, support may be necessary if a customer is to use and maintain properly the company's product. A company can benefit in two ways from providing service.

First, a company can preserve and enhance its reputation and its relationship with customers by providing guidance and support after a sale. This support may range from simply providing an operating manual to having a staff of service people on call, ready to address customer problems.

Second, this activity may prove to be an additional source of revenue. A car dealership may derive its primary revenue from sales, but an important secondary source of revenue may be the repair and service department.

In extreme instances, follow-up service may become the primary source of revenue. For example, a producer of photographic film might generate greater income from developing film than from selling it. Thus a company may wish to specify in its business plan the support it will offer its customers and the terms of such support.

Several points should be noted in reference to service and support and the role it may play in a new or emerging enterprise:

1. In the case of a new company, it may be preferable to contract the service function out rather than addressing it

in-house. This may help to reduce the cost and complexity of operations. Additionally, the use of a well-known and respected service organization may enhance the credibility of the new company in the market. This may have a direct and beneficial impact on the company's ability to sell and establish itself in the market.

2. The ability of the company to provide effective maintenance and service early in the lifetime of a product is especially important. It is during this initial period that customers will require the most guidance and also that there will be the highest incidence of product defect or failure. The company's ability to respond quickly in such instances will help solidify its position in the market. A negative impression created early in the product's life, due to the absence of necessary support and service, may prove difficult to overcome.

3. Proper service and support can be a way of establishing a continuing relationship with the customer. This, in turn, might be helpful later in the company's life as it develops new products and services and returns to its existing customer base as an important source of sales.

COMMENT: SERVICE AND SUPPORT

It should be noted that GFI does not directly address the question of customer service. This is a consequence of the nature of the product line, which requires little in the way of customer service.

GFI could have addressed service as it relates to distribution, such as delivery of product to distributors and display systems. However, the absence of a service section in this particular plan does not really present a problem.

While GFI addresses "services" in the marketing section of the plan, that discussion is of educational programs that are more promotion-oriented than customer-service oriented, strictly speaking.

OTHER INFLUENCES

Similar to a marketing plan, the operational plan should sometimes focus attention on external influences. Such influences almost always exist. It is up to the entrepreneur to decide which, if any, are important enough to discuss. These influences may take any one of a number of forms and may emanate from a variety of sources. Frequently, the entrepreneur has little or no control over these forces. While it is difficult to generalize in describing such influences, the following are some of them:

1. *Productive Resources.* Clearly, the manner in which a company operates will be dependent on the price and availability of productive resources such as labor and raw materials. Typically, such resources are subject to external influence. If the terms of acquiring a productive resource change materially, there may be a corresponding change in the company's operations.

For example, the price of a raw material might rise dramatically at the supplier's discretion, or because of political or economic instability where the material is found. This in turn might force the entrepreneur to utilize a different material.

Similarly, a hostile labor environment might create numerous work stoppages or an upward wage pressure. This might induce the entrepreneur to seek a less labor-intensive form of operation.

2. *Changing Technology.* The entrepreneur should be aware of the potential impact on the company of state-of-the-art changes and the likelihood of such changes. Similarly, competitive products might evolve in a manner that will have an impact on the company's operation.

For example, the introduction of new audio/video equipment might result in improved film quality. A studio utilizing older equipment might be vulnerable to this change in technology, which would render its facility less capable of producing high quality films.

3. *Customers.* The influence of customers might affect the manner in which a business operates. This is especially true where a company has a dominant customer or group of customers. The entrepreneur should address, where appropriate, influences emanating from the customer base.

4. *Regulation.* There is a maze of federal, state, and local guidelines that may have an impact on how a company operates. The Environmental Protection Agency (EPA) might prescribe a certain manner of waste disposal. A local community might have zoning ordinances that limit the company's activity. The Occupational Safety and Health Administration (OSHA) might have guidelines that have an impact on conditions in a particular work place. In any of these instances, the company's operations may be affected. These influences might also warrant attention in an operational plan.

In describing such influences the entrepreneur should, in a concise manner, address:

The nature and source of the influence.

The potential impact and the resulting risks or opportunities that are posed.

The manner in which the company may address the influence.

This is an area of the business plan that can have a profound effect internally on the company. Attention to the details of external influences can help reduce uncertainty and the risk of failure.

FDA REGULATION

The packaging of children's food is under the jurisdiction of the Food and Drug Administration (FDA). The manufacturer is required to follow FDA standards for canning and packaging. In addition, all labels, ingredient lists, and technical information must be registered with each state. Relations with these authorities will be handled by

Dr. Donald Schatzbert, an expert in this field, who is a member of GFI's advisory board.

COMMENT: OTHER INFLUENCES

This section is too brief and leaves a few important questions unanswered. What impact will regulation have on cost, liability, and innovation in the future?

PROTECTIONS

It is often appropriate to devote a brief section of the business plan to various forms of protection that have been or are being secured for products or processes. Possible protection includes patents, licenses, trademarks, or copyrights. Even when such protections are not anticipated to be a factor, comment to this effect is appropriate. Certainly, many companies have thrived without the benefit of a patent or license, but they are often very helpful.

These forms of protection do not only apply to high technology and state-of-the-art products. A company may secure a license to be the exclusive distributor of a product.

In addition, it is important to note that these protections do not apply only to the ultimate product or service. The process for manufacturing a product might be patented. Or a single feature of a multidimensional product may be patented.

The benefit of such protection is clear. It may permit the possessor to have and maintain some competitive advantage for a period of time. This can be especially important in the case of an early-stage business. On the other hand, the competitive advantage provided may be marginal or nonexistent.

In the context of a business plan, patents, licenses, and other forms of protection should be addressed from a number of perspectives. This section should make clear the benefits and associated areas of concern resulting from these protections.

Inherent risks must also be considered, such as what might happen if a license agreement is terminated. These issues may be treated in the following manner:

1. *What Is Being Protected.* This must be specifically defined. There are numerous forms of protection and each form may apply to a single attribute or a range of attributes, from a product feature to an entire product or an entire line of products. In defining this, the entrepreneur should explain where he or she is in the process of securing protection. For example, he or she might be in the process of negotiating a licensing agreement, or may have already negotiated this agreement, with the agreement being effective at some point in the future. Or, the agreement might already be negotiated and in force.

2. *Impact of Protection.* It is then necessary to describe, in practical terms, the impact of the protection. There are instances when this impact will be profound, making probable a long-term competitive advantage. There are also instances where the impact will be minimal or nonexistent.

For example, a company has patented a product or process that is already less than state-of-the-art. In such a case, it is not necessary to include any detail about it in the business plan.

In most instances, however, the impact of protection is somewhere between the extremes, where the real advantage is seen in the "head start" a venture gains prior to the appearance of competitive goods and processes. A business plan may assert, for example, that its patented product will be the only one of its kind in the immediate future and that no competitive products are expected to appear in the next 24 months.

3. *Documentation.* In an instance where the impact of a patent, license, or other protection is expected to be substantial, there is a strong possibility that a prospective lender or investor will want to review legal documentation. It is not appropriate to include voluminous legal documentation in a business plan. It can be mentioned, however, that an examination of

legal documents, agreements, and related material is possible at the request of the reviewer.

In many business plans, a section focusing on patents, licenses, and other potential forms of protection is relatively unimportant, simply because the company has not secured such protection. In instances where such protection has been or is being sought, however, this brief section can be critical in communicating a substantial portion of the venture's attractiveness.

PROTECTIONS

The specific techniques used in the GFI manufacturing process are proprietary, but not patentable. They will only be released to a few selected processors, who will be required to sign nondisclosure, noncompete agreements.

COMMENT: PROTECTIONS

Here again, GFI is far too brief and does not discuss the impact of the protection on cost, appeal of the product, the ability of others to copy or at least imitate the products since there are no protections, and how long a head start GFI has on those who would like to imitate.

It should also be noted that this is not the only section in the business plan where "protection" might be discussed. It could also be in the marketing or products and services section.

10

MANAGEMENT AND ORGANIZATION

It is not unusual for a business plan reviewer to read the personnel and organization section early in the review process. No matter how exciting the business concept, most reviewers are reluctant to make any kind of commitment to a venture unless they are comfortable with those involved in it. Venture capitalists have often commented that they invest in management teams, not in ideas or products. Success in generating the interest of reviewers and the ultimate success of the business often depend on effective staff and organization.

Many ventures ultimately fail because the proper talent has not been assembled. Individuals with strong technical backgrounds might ignore the importance of including on a management team people with the appropriate business background, and vice versa.

In order to properly address this issue, the entrepreneur must begin with an objective assessment of his or her personal strengths and weaknesses, and an assessment of the company's requirements. Based on these assessments, the composition of the rest of the company may be defined. In turn, the entrepreneur will also define the company's personality. A number of questions need to be addressed:

Will management be participative or autocratic?

Will personnel share in the company's financial success, or be treated more as a commodity?

Will responsibilities and tasks be sharply defined, or will a more flexible approach prevail?

The following issues must be treated:

1. *Management Team/Principals.* One of the most important parts of the business plan, and certainly the most important part of the personnel and organization section, is a presentation of the backgrounds of those individuals expected to play key roles in the initiation and operation of the venture. This group might include the entrepreneur(s), investors, members of the board of directors, key employees, or almost anyone who will have a significant impact on the company's ultimate success or failure.

2. *Organizational Chart.* After introducing the key participants in the venture, it is appropriate to offer an organizational chart that presents the relationships and divisions of responsibility within the organization. In some instances a brief narrative instead of, or in addition to, a chart may be helpful in providing further detail.

3. *Policy and Strategy.* The business plan should include a statement as to how employees will be selected, trained, and rewarded. Such background can be important for reviewers to give them a feel for the company's style. A brief reference to the type of benefits and incentives planned may further help define the company's spirit.

A somewhat overused but nonetheless accurate statement often made by businesspeople is, "Our greatest asset is our people." This is especially true in the case of a start-up or early-stage company, where errors in judgment and operations are often magnified because of a lack of stability and resources.

MANAGEMENT TEAM/PRINCIPALS

Business plan reviewers need to feel comfortable that those on the management team are not just bright and motivated, but that they can transform their business plan into a successful operating entity.

The first decision to make when preparing this part of the business plan is who should be featured. The business plan should feature those who will play a significant role in the venture and, secondarily, those who will lend credibility to the venture in the reviewer's eyes. Among those often meriting attention are:

1. *Founding Entrepreneurs.* In almost every instance it is appropriate to include information about the individuals responsible for conceptualizing, starting, and running the venture—at least in the early stages. The importance of these people should be evident and requires little comment.

2. *Active Investors.* On occasion, there may be reason to devote attention to those who have made a significant commitment of capital and who will also provide expertise and direction on a full-time or peripheral basis. It is usually not necessary to include comments on passive investors, since their abilities are seldom brought to bear on the success or failure of the business.

3. *Key Employees.* There may be individuals who do not have an equity stake in the venture, but whose talent has an important influence on the business. This group might include a marketing director, technical director, or plant manager.

If these people are crucial to the venture and if they do not have an equity stake in it, there may be good reason to secure their commitment to the venture via some form of employment contract. Such a commitment could be important to both the entrepreneur and the reviewer.

4. *Directors.* There may be some individuals who will contribute their services on a part-time basis, but who nonetheless will have an impact on the company's operations. Directors have a formal, legal relationship with the company, and a fiduciary responsibility to it.

5. *Advisory Board.* Many new companies turn to an advisory board for assistance in technical, planning, marketing,

operations, or other matters. Lenders and investors both like to see that an entrepreneur is willing to ask advice, does not think he or she knows all the answers, and has created a formal system to make sure he or she doesn't fall into the isolation that can sometimes happen when someone is consumed with getting a business off the ground. The credentials of advisory board members can also add credibility to a venture.

6. *Key Advisors.* These are usually individuals who have special relationships with the entrepreneurial team, but don't sit on the formal advisory board. They can include lawyers, accountants, and consultants in any or all facets of a business.

Once a determination has been made as to who should be introduced in this part of the business plan, the next decision is what background to present. There is a good deal of flexibility in this regard.

Sometimes it is enough to include carefully prepared resumes detailing the background and achievements of each member of the team. In other instances, more detail is appropriate and can be offered in the form of concise narrative biographies. Because credibility is often a key objective, supplementary material such as flattering articles or lists of honors and achievements may be included, either in this section or as an appendix.

Several caveats must be made at this point:

1. While a management team associated with a long list of failures is obviously disconcerting, the entrepreneur need not present an absolutely spotless record to the reviewer. In fact, some lenders and investors will view as a benefit the ability to perform under adverse conditions.

At least one venture capitalist has remarked he prefers an individual who has experienced failure because such a person is more likely to recognize limitations and consider valuable judgments from others.

As a consequence, the aspiring entrepreneur who has "tasted defeat" should not assume that this background will necessarily repel lenders and investors.

2. As important as the management team and principals are, all the talent in the world cannot turn a terrible concept into a successful business. Some reviewers take the attitude that a good business concept is a given for any venture they invest in, but ineffective leadership can be replaced. In fact, such leadership often is replaced if the venture does not perform up to expectations.

3. As a practical matter, a prospective member of the management team may not want his or her name used if he or she is currently involved in another position. This can create obvious difficulties if such an individual is key to the perceived probability of success. One way to address the problem is to present this person's background without identifying the person. For instance, write: "Our chief financial officer has spent the last five years as vice-president of a regional investment bank . . ."

VII. MANAGEMENT AND ORGANIZATION

This section of the business plan outlines GFI's key management personnel, the company's major outside advisors in the health food areas, as well as legal counsel, accounting and financial advisors, marketing consultants, and the company's expected organization.

Top Management

The company's three principals are:

Judith M. Appel	**President/marketing director**
George P. Knapp, MD	**Research director**
Samuel Knapp, MD	**Consultant**

Each of these individuals brings unique competence to the GFI venture.

Ms. Appel is a nutritionist with experience in marketing and retailing of health food products, and is co-founder of GFI.

For the last six years she has run Nature's Best, Inc., a store in Great Neck, New York, specializing in the sale of natural food and health-care products. For the last 14 months, the NBI store was used to test the idea of health products for children, and to offer the consumer one-stop shopping for all of the family's health foods and health-care products.

Drs. George and Samuel Knapp are physicians specializing in pediatrics, and are co-founders of GFI. Both have had a long-standing interest in holistic treatment of children. Their practices have relied heavily on the use of natural curative and preventive medicines.

The doctors have been pioneers in the area of naturally derived foods, supplements, and techniques for treating children. Recently, both doctors have limited their involvement in their pediatric practices to devote more time and effort to the company's operations.

George Knapp will serve as a full-time employee of the company, while Samuel Knapp will serve as a consultant. Their resumes are included in Attachment A.

The other members of the management team are discussed in the following section on organization and personnel.

Ownership

The ownership of the company prior to raising additional capital is as follows:

	Shares (%)
Judith M. Appel	31
George P. Knapp, MD	31
Samuel Knapp, MD	31
Other investors	7

Technical Advisory Board

In addition to the three principals, GFI has a technical advisory board of individuals experienced in the care and feeding of children and the holistic approach to nutrition. Among them are:

Otto Vladnick, PhD

Dr. Vladnick received his PhD in nutrition, biochemistry, and physiology from the University of Illinois. He is well known in the field of child nutrition as a consultant and problem solver. He has lectured for pediatric associations both in the United States and Canada. Dr. Vladnick was previously employed with Armour and Co. and the American Meat Institution Foundation as director of nutrition. He is currently a consultant to Ethical Data Laboratories and M^2 Productions Co., Chicago, Illinois, which develops nutritional supplements.

Mac Farland, PhD

Dr. Farland received his PhD in nutrition from North Dakota State University. He was employed as director of nutritional services and new Product development at Children's Foods by Olympia Valley Farms, Inc., New Brunswick, New Jersey. He is currently president and chief operating officer of Resource Management, Inc. of Southport, Pennsylvania.

Margaret Vallum

Ms. Vallum was educated in Pennsylvania and is now a certified herbalist. As a consultant to the herb and natural food industry she has researched and developed products and written articles, pamphlets, and a book entitled *Cooking with Sea Vegetables*. Currently, she is lecturing and educating while expanding her business to include health and herbal books, charts, and workshops.

Zina Johnson, MD

Dr. Johnson is head of the Department of Clinical Nutrition at Iowa State University School of Medicine. She has been a paid consultant to GFI since its inception. Her involvement ensures that GFI's holistic concepts are acceptable and compatible with conventional nutritional data.

Donald Schatzbert, MD

Dr. Schatzbert served as chief of pediatric services at Heights Hospital for Children for 20 years. He then acted as a liaison between the FDA and three local hospital boards. He currently assists GFI in adhering to all FDA regulations.

Mark Eichen, MD
Dr. Eichen is a conventional pediatrician practicing in New York City. His participation ensures that GFI's pediatric information is acceptable and compatible with conventional medicine.

Business and Legal Advisors

In addition to these specialists, GFI has also identified key professional advisors. They include:

Marketing
Marketing expertise will be provided by *Vick Products Sales Research Corporation* of Greenwich, Connecticut, which specializes in market development services for new ventures. The Company has proven itself to be unique because of its ability to identify market niches, design realistic and workable marketing plans, and follow programs through implementation. The founders were the managing team behind Perrier's and Chipwich's introductions in New York City.

Legal
The general counsel for GFI is Smith, Jones and Howe, PC. The patent and trademark attorneys are the firm of Gottlieb, Schwartz and Fine, PC. Both firms are located in New York City and have experience with food companies and FDA activities.

Accounting and Finance
Accounting and financial services will be provided by Ernst & Young Entrepreneurial Services Group.

COMMENT: MANAGEMENT

GFI successfully leaps the first key hurdle that will be posed in the review process by presenting a credible group of principals and advisors.

The three principals all appear to be experts in their field. The company has also assembled a distinguished advisory board. This is not unusual, and can be helpful in "beefing up" this section of the plan.

Of course, active participation by these advisors would have a positive impact on the company. However, their mere willingness to be named as advisors helps to confer credibility. Similarly, the use of professionals experienced with entrepreneurial companies enhances credibility.

The single notable flaw in the team is that little emphasis is placed on any previous entrepreneurial success. While this is not a fatal flaw, the presence of such experience is valuable in starting a new company and in selling a lender or investor on the merits of the deal.

ORGANIZATIONAL CHART

Typically, there are only a few individuals involved in the early stages of planning and implementing a venture. As a consequence, a premium is often placed on flexibility and the entrepreneur's ability to address diverse problems. Regardless of this, even during these initial stages it is important that a blueprint for the company's organizational development be clearly identified. In most circumstances, this plan is depicted in the form of an organizational chart.

In order to prepare such a chart in an effective manner, the entrepreneur must address several issues:

1. Both the company's immediate needs and those that will become important as the business evolves need to be identified.

2. It is necessary to identify the kinds of individuals required to address such responsibilities.

3. Attention must be given to interrelationships among these individuals and how tasks will be assigned to them.

This will result in a definition of the company's organizational structure. Though such planning should be done in a detailed manner, the organizational chart presented in the business plan generally does not require a fine level of detail. In instances where detail beyond a simple chart is warranted, some brief narrative might be included in order to enhance the reviewer's understanding.

Clearly, the precise form of organization will vary from business to business. But for the most part businesses will be organized either by product or by function; that is, employees will be working on product *a*, product *b*, and so forth, or employees will be working in the marketing department, financial department, and so on. Some businesses may use a hybrid of the two approaches, a matrix where people cross over from functions to work on specific products or projects.

Clearly, the company's organization should be structured in a manner that allows tasks and responsibilities to be addressed in the most effective manner.

The entrepreneur needs to show particular care in the following respects:

There should be a good deal of consistency between the development of an organizational chart and the rest of the business plan. Strategies and methods emphasized in other parts of the plan should be embodied in this chart.

While at the outset it may be necessary and beneficial for the entrepreneur(s) to embrace a great many activities and become familiar with all aspects of the company, eventually growth will necessitate formal organization. Too often, entrepreneurs are unable to delegate and organize effectively. The result may be that a thriving $500,000 business grows into a sluggish, unprofitable, $5 million business.

The first, and sometimes most sensitive, organizational decisions occur when there is more than one founder and attention must be focused on how responsibilities and, more importantly, authority will be divided. Such questions should be resolved early in the venture's development to promote a harmonious and effective management team.

ORGANIZATIONAL CHART

Initially, GFI will operate with a small staff that will include the three principals whose backgrounds and qualifications have been outlined. They will be assisted by a sales manager and a secretary/bookkeeper. The anticipated positions and salaries are:

Name	Position	Salary
Judith Appel	President/marketing director	$70,000
George Knapp, MD	Research Director	$60,000
Mark Livingston	Sales manager	$45,000
Carrie Jurish	Secretary/bookkeeper	$20,000
Samuel Knapp, MD	Consultant	Day rate

Since GFI will initially target its sales efforts at a limited number of distributors, a limited sales force is projected. By the third year, when another market is entered, GFI will hire an assistant sales manager. A full-time marketing director will be brought on during the second year in preparation for expansion. GFI also intends to hire a treasurer/controller in the second year. Other personnel will be added as necessary.

COMMENT: ORGANIZATIONAL CHART

As basic as the organization is, some mention should be made of how new activities will be organized and how the organization will be developed in the future. A clearer picture of orderly development is necessary.

POLICY AND STRATEGY

The policy and strategy section is not meant to serve as a personnel manual. Such a level of detail would be counterproductive. However, it should communicate the philosophy guiding the company's organization and staffing. In large part, this helps to give some insight into the company's personality. While decisions related to this issue might not have an immediate and direct impact on the prospects for success, they will have an important impact on the company's long-term effectiveness.

Some of the important factors to consider are:

1. *Timing*. Early in a venture's development, there is frequently good reason to maintain as low a level of expenses as possible, since at this point there is often little, if any, internally generated capital. It is therefore important to plan carefully exactly how and when to begin staffing. In some instances there may be sufficient certainty to create a schedule of the organization's evolution for the first few years.

2. *Selection*. Ineffective selection procedures and guidelines are problematic no matter how young or old the company is. However, making the appropriate hiring decision is especially critical in a company's early life. Early-stage ventures frequently do not have a second chance to correct blunders. As a consequence, there is a premium on bringing in capable personnel at the outset. Thus attention to hiring standards and procedures is often appropriate in a business plan.

3. *Compensation*. It is often worthwhile to include brief descriptions of employee compensation. While an actual payroll schedule is not critical, it is of interest to some reviewers for the entrepreneur to touch on issues such as salary structure relative to competition, benefits packages, bonus and incentive plans, profit sharing, stock options, and similar items. It might also be of interest to comment on how these compensation policies will evolve over time.

In far too many instances, policy and strategy considerations as they relate to personnel are ignored in a business plan. In a sense, this is understandable, since such considerations do not have immediate and direct impact on the venture's prospects. Despite this rationale, however, these issues are important in the long term, particularly if significant growth is being sought.

ANTICIPATED YEAR OF INITIAL HIRINGS

		1	2	3	4	5
Administration						
President	$70,000	X				
Treasurer/controller	$60,000		X			
Secretary 1	$20,000	X				
Secretary 2	$20,000			X		
Bookkeeper	$20,000	X				
Delivery person	$15,000			X		
Research and Development						
R&D director	$60,000	X				
Assistant	$25,000			X		
Sales and Marketing						
Marketing director	$45,000		X			
National sales manager						
(begins second quarter)	$45,000	X				
Assistant	$25,000			X		
Assistant	$25,000					X
Premix Production						
Three premix producers	$18,000 each	X				

COMMENT: HIRING AND SALARY

GFI is very specific as to whom it will hire, how much the company will pay these employees, and when they will be hired. The schedule the company presents is concise and complete.

However, the company says little about compensation strategy or philosophy. This is particularly important as it relates to retaining the key personnel over a period of time—particularly such people as the controller and marketing director.

Incentive plans such as profit sharing or stock options may be integral to the company's ability to attract talented people (particularly in early years when cash is tight). As a result, attention to compensation strategy is warranted in GFI's plan.

11

MAJOR MILESTONES

It is important to place plans and objectives for a venture into some sort of time frame. From the reviewer's perspective, this information allows for a more accurate assessment of the venture's attractiveness. From the entrepreneur's perspective, such a framework represents both a schedule and set of goals against which progress can be measured.

The major milestones section of the business plan is intended to present this time frame. This section should identify major events in the venture's development and when they are likely to occur.

It is usually advisable to offer dates in a generic manner rather than by the actual calendar in order not to give the impression of being behind schedule.

This schedule should focus only on major events, although more detailed calendars, PERT charts, or other schedules might be prepared for internal planning purposes. Major events in the development of a new venture include such things as financing commitments, prototype development, a first market test, the initiation of production and sales, attaining break-even performance, and expanding operations.

What is important and what is not important depends on the nature of the venture. For example, site selection and negotiation of a lease may be crucial in a service-oriented business, but have far less significance to a manufacturing company.

It is sometimes appropriate to address in this section events that have already occurred, so that the reviewer understands how quickly the venture has developed to the point of the preparation of the business plan.

For planning purposes, it is valuable to prepare far more detailed schedules for use as time-and-action or implementation calendars. These would not ordinarily be included in the presented business plan. This detail will help the entrepreneur determine a realistic plan of progress for the venture. It will help ensure a smooth and orderly implementation of the strategies and activities communicated in the business plan. Good plans sometimes fail because of a lack of attention to detail.

A few practical points worth considering are as follows:

Progress will occur more slowly than anticipated, particularly when the cooperation of an external individual or organization is necessary. While the venture may be of paramount importance to the entrepreneur, it is likely to be far less important to such people as the venture capitalist, lender, vendor, or lawyer. As a consequence, "unnecessary" delays are probable.

An adequate margin of comfort should always be left in planning. Approach financing sources well in advance of financial requirements and allow for delays in the delivery and installation of equipment.

In preparing a schedule of major milestones, offer a schedule that is ambitious but can be met or exceeded. This way the entrepreneur can develop a reputation for achieving objectives, which will enhance credibility in the future.

One should select milestones that can be clearly defined and easily measured. While "design 50-percent complete" is vague and difficult to assess, "first customer delivery" has far more meaning.

GFI does not define its major milestones' other than the overview statement made in the executive summary. Although it is not necessary to have a detailed statement of milestones, it would be worth reiterating that executive summary statement here, especially for the reviewers who are making a second pass at the plan after having examined the summary separately. By omitting a statement of major milestones, GFI loses an opportunity to underline the timely manner in which it expects to proceed.

═══ 12 ═══

STRUCTURE AND CAPITALIZATION

It is in the structure and capitalization section that the business plan allows the entrepreneur to say to a reviewer: "You've reviewed my business plan. If you are interested here's what the business requires."

This is where the entrepreneur identifies what legal form will be selected and how the venture will be capitalized. Typically, this section is concise and precise, although there are also occasions where some detail should deliberately be omitted.

In a planning sense, this is one of the most critical parts of the proposal. It is at this point that the entrepreneur must convey what kind of financial resources are required in order for the venture to succeed during its early life. A venture that begins life undercapitalized has a staggering handicap.

While it is difficult enough to run a business properly when adequate resources are available, a scarcity of resources renders such an endeavor significantly more difficult. Conversely, raising excess capital is also undesirable, because in order to do so one frequently must give up more equity in one's company or assume more debt service.

In general, this part of the business plan should be organized as follows:

1. *Structure.* There are a number of decisions to be made in devising a company's appropriate structure. The two most

critical choices are legal form and manner of financial participation.

With regard to legal form, an entrepreneur must decide whether the venture is to be a sole proprietorship, partnership, limited partnership, subchapter S corporation, or corporation. This has been addressed in greater detail in Chapter 3.

2. *Capital Requirements.* At this juncture of the business plan, some outline of the present sources of funds, and those that are expected in the future, is necessary so the potential source of funding can understand how the investment or loan fits into the business's overall financial picture.

It is important to tell potential financing sources how much money the entrepreneur(s) have invested in the venture, how much they may have loaned the company, and about all other sources of funding. In addition, it is necessary to tell potential funding sources what other sources will be approached—for example, investors need to know how much future borrowing will be necessary.

The entrepreneur has a wide variety of options to offer his or her capital providers for their participation. He or she may offer equity, debt, or hybrids such as convertible debt (debt that can be converted into equity). Some of these alternatives offer fixed rates of return, while others hold the promise of returns that vary with the company's performance. Certain forms of participation permit providers of capital an active voice in the company's affairs, while in other instances only a limited voice or no voice at all is offered.

Among the most commonly offered forms of participation, moving along a continuum from debt to simple equity, are:

1. *Term Loans.* These are instruments used to acquire a fixed sum of money, with principal and interest repaid over a defined period of time. The interest rate can either be fixed or floating, although usually in today's volatile credit market the

rate floats for new or small companies. The loan amount is usually secured by the borrower's collateral.

2. *Line of Credit.* This is usually a working capital financing agreement that allows the borrower to maintain a fluctuating debt balance. The interest rate fluctuates in the market, therefore there should be enough collateral to cover the maximum debt allowed on the credit line. Sometimes the maximum balance available on the loan is tied to a specific measurable sum, such as a percentage of accounts receivable.

3. *Convertible Bond.* Convertible bonds are a common form of "hybrid security." They are debt securities issued by a corporation to creditors called bondholders. The convertibility option allows a bondholder to convert the bond into a specified number of shares of stock (usually common stock) in the company issuing the bond. The time period within which the conversion is allowed to take place is usually limited.

Convertible bonds often allow management to raise capital at the lowest possible cost, since interest rates on convertible debt are often lower than interest on straight bonds. This is because the convertibility factor allows lenders to attain the capital gain benefits of investors if they convert their bonds to stock.

A "call" provision written into a convertible debt allows the issuing company to redeem the bond at an appreciated value, often within a defined period of time. Conversely, a "put" provision allows the bondholder to redeem the bond at an agreed upon value, also often within a defined period of time.

4. *Bond Issued With a Stock Warrant.* This is another hybrid security. It is a bond sold with another instrument—a warrant—that allows the bondholder to purchase a defined number of shares (usually of common stock) at a designated price during a defined time period. Warrants can be separated from the bond, and in the case of public companies can be traded in the open market.

This financing method also allows management to finance at a lower cost, because bonds issued with warrants often pay lower interest rates than straight bonds. Again, lenders are able to become investors and reap the capital gain benefits.

A call provision allows the issuer to redeem the warrant at an appreciated value, while a put provision allows the bondholder to force the issuer to redeem the warrant, again usually at an appreciated value.

5. *Preferred Stock.* Preferred stock is an equity instrument that maintains dividend rights over ordinary common stock and collects a steady dividend, fixed as a percentage of the market price.

6. *Cumulative Preferred Stock.* This is an equity instrument that contains the provision that if a dividend is not paid in one year, the dividend obligation carries forward until it is fully distributed in subsequent years.

7. *Convertible Preferred Stock.* These equity instruments contain the provision that the preferred stock may be converted into common stock at the stockholder's option.

A call provision allows the issuer to redeem the stock at an appreciated value, while a put provision allows the holder to force the issuer to redeem the stock at an agreed-upon value.

Convertibility allows the stockholders to enjoy the security of preferred stock along with the higher potential capital gains available to common-stock holders.

8. *Common Stock.* Common stock is an equity instrument which is used to secure capital in return for a share in the corporation. Here stock value varies directly with the market value of the company. There are two types of common stock:

Voting stock, whose holders maintain rights to have a say in company affairs

Nonvoting stock, whose holders have no such say.

STRUCTURING THE DEAL

Structuring a deal—both with respect to the best form a business should take and to how capital sources should participate—is one of the areas of entrepreneurship where professional advice should be sought. With this in mind, we have three suggestions:

1. The entrepreneur should find good, trusted lawyers and accountants to explore the issues of liability, taxes, and related matters. Entrepreneurs often feel they are in a "Catch-22" situation; they can't afford the best professional advice, but they feel they can't afford to be without it for the long-term good of the venture. Many professional advisors are willing to "work with" entrepreneurs, however. They will do such things as reduce rates, defer billing, or in special cases even work in exchange for an equity stake in a venture. Entrepreneurs should not feel embarrassed about initiating these kinds of discussions and negotiations.

2. The entrepreneur should be careful to avoid negotiating in the business plan. For example, the entrepreneur who indicates he or she will sell 20 percent of the company for $200,000 has just established the upper end of the negotiating range. Sophisticated reviewers will realize that at worst they can acquire 20 percent of the venture for $200,000, and that they might be able to negotiate a better price.

3. In general, the entrepreneur should avoid complicated structures. Often, too many participants or too many forms of participation allow opportunity for breakdown. A simple, straightforward plan is frequently the most effective.

Thus the entrepreneur must take care in devising a structure for the deal, and then demonstrate equal care in communicating its details. It should be recognized that during the planning and negotiations, it is likely that this structure will undergo some change.

CAPITAL REQUIREMENTS

Accurately determining a venture's capital requirements generally involves a combination of investigation and intuition, as well as a degree of luck in forecasting future events that will ultimately have an impact on the level of capital required.

The easiest place for the entrepreneur to start is with the capital required for the acquisition of tangible assets such as equipment, inventory, and real estate. Here the entrepreneur must identify what is required and seek out cost quotations, estimates, and agreements of sale in order to translate each requirement into an anticipated cost. Depending on the reviewer's desires, documentation may or may not be included in the business plan. However, regardless of whether this documentation is included, the entrepreneur must go through the steps of gathering it, in order to feel comfortable in his projections.

It is more difficult to project working and contingent capital requirements. In large part, these requirements are a function of projected cash flow, which will be discussed more closely in the financial plan (Chapter 13). The entrepreneur must have sufficient capital available to address initial shortfalls in cash projections, and then some additional capital in order to provide for deviations from expected financial performance and unanticipated problems and opportunities. Precisely how much capital of this kind is required is not easy to project. Because of this, it is normally better for the entrepreneur to err on the high side than the low side.

As a final note, the entrepreneur's projected requirement should be consistent with the rest of the plan. For example, if there is a likelihood of unexpected opportunity and a need to react swiftly to such opportunity, an appropriate level of contingent capital should be available. Similarly, if the venture is attempting to develop a new product line and there is great uncertainty as to when revenue will first be generated, adequate provision should be made when projecting a working capital requirement. Obviously, there should be conformity between the numbers offered in this section and those included in the financial plan—especially those on the balance sheet, since a balance sheet directly reflects sources of capital and how that capital has been applied.

SOURCES OF CAPITAL

After specifying uses of capital, it is necessary for the entrepreneur to identify prospective sources of capital.

Rule one in this regard is that sources and uses of capital must be equal in amount.

Rule two, as previously mentioned, is not to negotiate in the business plan.

The entrepreneur may offer a general description of the capital sources, such as "$200,000 will be raised in the form of equity."

The entrepreneur must research potential sources closely. A particular venture capital fund might be reluctant to invest in a start-up. Or a bank might require a certain degree of equity participation before it will contribute debt capital. An entrepreneur, at best, wastes time by submitting a business plan to a source that has no interest in it.

The entrepreneur also needs to have at least a basic understanding of how a particular source evaluates a deal before approaching that source. This will allow presentation of the business plan in a favorable manner.

Additionally, the entrepreneur should consider the personalities involved at the source of the financing. The relationship with a lender or investor may be long term and the entrepreneur may have to interact with him or her in difficult as well as prosperous times.

When approaching a potential source of financing, the following guidelines are useful:

Get an introduction if possible from one of your advisors such as your lawyer, accountant, consultant banker or someone from your advisiory board. It is more difficult to interest a reviewer whom you approach cold than one who is approached via a supportive introduction. Using such an intermediary helps to draw attention to your plan and lends it credibility.

Be selective. A mass mailing of business plans is usually not a productive course. A more advisable strategy is to approach attractive sources of capital selectively and focus attention on each.

Be prepared to rethink a plan. If the entrepreneur receives consistently negative responses to a business plan, it may suggest a problem with the plan rather than a consequence of not approaching enough or the right sources. In this instance, listen to sources' objections to the plan and reevaluate it.

Some sources want to see a summary of a business plan—perhaps the executive summary—rather than the entire plan, in order to facilitate their preliminary evaluation.

When a deal has been structured with the anticipated participation of more than one source, the review can be expedited by having the sources review the plan concurrently.

It is not enough to simply identify the appropriate financing organization. The entrepreneur must be careful to identify the appropriate individual within the organization. A large lending organization may have several departments capable of reviewing a business plan. In the same way, a venture capitalist may have specialists in different types or stages of business.

Raising capital can be a stressful, time-consuming activity. It is easy for the entrepreneur to make the mistake of focusing all of his or her attention on this stage of the venture when, in fact, the real battle is not begun until after financing has been arranged. Regardless, raising capital often represents the first serious obstacle to the entrepreneur. As a consequence, he or she must be effective in this effort if the venture is to have a chance of succeeding.

VIII. STRUCTURE AND CAPITALIZATION

Based on the detailed analysis of GFI's projected financial results presented in the next section, the company projects a need for $700,000 in equity investment.

These funds will be used to finance the initial marketing effort, to complete the development and testing of other products, and to provide sufficient working capital for the company as it begins operations.

The terms of this transaction are subject to negotiation.

Funds will be used as follows:

Initial marketing campaign	$363,000
Product development and testing	125,000
Working capital	212,000
Total	$700,000

COMMENT: STRUCTURE AND CAPITALIZATION

GFI presents a concise picture of its capital requirements. Astutely, it does not establish a negotiating point. It simply mentions that the level of equity participation to be gained by the investor is subject to negotiation.

The deal is structured as an equity infusion, and rightly so. The $700,000 is not buying any tangible assets and thus would offer a lender practically no security.

There is one significant omission here. If one reviews the projected cash flow in Chapter 13 it is clear that the requested capital (including working capital) is not enough to avert cash shortfalls in years two and three.

Reference is made to "short-term borrowing" in the cash flow projections. GFI should identify the source of this borrowing in this section. Also, in the absence of any significant debt relationship, little provision has been made for future contingent or growth capital.

Finally, at no point does GFI state what the company's legal form is. We know, from the business plan's title, that it is a corporation, but not if it is an S corporation, or where it is incorporated.

13

FINANCIAL PLAN

The purpose of the financial section of a business plan is to formulate a credible, comprehensive set of projections reflecting the company's anticipated financial performance. If these projections are carefully prepared and convincingly supported, they become one of the most critical yardsticks by which the business's attractiveness is measured.

While the rest of the business plan communicates a basic understanding of the nature of the enterprise, projected financial performance addresses itself most directly to the bottom-line interests and concerns of both the entrepreneur and the reviewer. It is here that the investor discovers what sort of return he or she should anticipate, and the lender learns about the borrower's capacity to service debt.

In the case of a new or infant enterprise, it is important to put the nature of the financial plan into proper perspective. In such a situation, there is no financial history on which one may base estimates. The obvious consequence is that projections will be clouded with uncertainty. However, while the financial section of such a business plan will explore a less-than-certain future, attention to detail can make this section far better than guesswork.

First, one can't overemphasize the importance of reliable data. The quality of research is directly reflected in the accuracy of projections. Further, the reviewer will likely do his or her own investigation and evaluation in order to assess the validity of these projections. The implication is that if the financial section deviates from appropriate guidelines, such as industry averages or ratios, there had better be a sound explanation of why that is so.

Second, because it is widely accepted that projected financial analysis will be to some extent uncertain, it is often advisable to calculate more than one financial scenario, even if all of these scenarios are not presented in the formal plan. As in the marketing plan, the financial plan might include several sets of projections—for example, one based on a conservative set of assumptions and another reflecting the business's full potential. Together these projections become a framework, or sensitivity analysis, allowing the reviewer a better understanding of the company's anticipated performance.

Third, it is important to review periodically, and, when appropriate, revise projections. A lender or investor may examine a business plan over many weeks or months. During this period, significant events might occur that have an impact on expected financial performance. For example, certain contracts may have been awarded that result in anticipation of greater sales volume. Or the price of raw materials might change, influencing expected gross profit. If a business plan is to be effective as a planning tool and as a document used to raise financing, its content must be current. This is especially true of financial projections.

Fourth, the financial plan must conform to the details presented in the remainder of the business plan. If the marketing section presents an elaborate and expensive advertising campaign, this should be reflected in the projected income statement. If a seasonal pattern has been indicated in a sales analysis, projected cash flow should incorporate the same pattern. A lack of consistency will indicate either carelessness or an incomplete understanding of the business.

In many respects, the financial plan is the least flexible part of a business plan in terms of format. While actual numbers will vary, each plan should contain similar statements—or schedules—and each statement should be presented in a conventional manner. There should be enough information in these statistics to let reviewers know that the entrepreneur understands not only his or her particular business, but how it relates to similar businesses.

Circumstances will dictate to some degree the detail of the financial statistics presented. Some companies keep records annually, and others quarterly, monthly, weekly, or even daily. But in general, the information that should be presented includes the following:

The set of assumptions on which projections are based should be clearly and concisely presented. Numbers without these assumptions will have little meaning. It is only after carefully considering such assumptions that the reviewer will be able to assess the validity of financial projections. Because the rest of the financial plan is an outgrowth of the assumptions, they are, in an important sense, the most integral part of this section.

Projected income statements, typically for five years and for at least three years, should be included. These statements most often reflect at least quarterly performance for the first two years, while years three through five are often quarterly or annual.

Projected cash flow statements for the first two years should be developed in as great a detail as possible. Quarterly or annual cash flows, corresponding to the period used for the income statements, are sufficient for years three through five.

A current balance sheet—for new companies, a balance sheet reflecting the financial position of the company at its inception—and projected year-end balance sheets, typically for five years and for at least three years, should be included.

Other financial projections might also be helpful. For example, a break-even analysis will demonstrate the level of sales required to break even at a given scale of operation. Additionally, financial summaries that reflect the contribution of specific products and services to overall company performance might be prepared.

In addition, it is appropriate to include historical financial performance for an existing business looking to expand or acquire another company. Depending on the business's age and nature, a reviewer will generally want three or more years of income statements and balance sheets. Also, depending on when the most recent fiscal year ended, the reviewer may require interim financial statements, perhaps as of the conclusion of the most recent quarter.

The financial plan, properly prepared, can be used to assess performance after the business actually starts. In some instances this plan may be the basis for a detailed operating budget. Here again, the purpose of a business plan goes beyond the review by interested, external parties. It actually becomes a guiding document, detailing how and when capital should be expended and listing objectives that must be achieved if the business is to be successful.

IX. FINANCIAL DATA

The following schedules, which have not been audited or reviewed by an independent CPA, provide detailed financial projections for years one through five of GFI's operation. These projections represent management's best estimates of future financial performance.

In summary, GFI expects to have a positive cash flow within the first quarter of year four and to be profitable throughout that year. By the end of year six, the company anticipates operating at a 50 percent gross profit margin; a 9.6 percent of sales after-tax profit with a return on equity of 48.9 percent.

Attached are the following schedules:

Notes and assumptions for financial projections

Projected statement of operations (income statements)

Summary of historical financial data

Current estimated balance sheet

Projected cash flow statements

Projected balance sheets

Estimates of selected financial ratios and statistics

NOTES AND ASSUMPTIONS FOR FINANCIAL PROJECTIONS

The importance of assumptions in relation to the overall financial section has already been emphasized. Without them, it is almost impossible for the reviewer to assess the projections competently. The guiding objectives in presenting assumptions is to be compelling yet concise.

The reviewer probably will not have the same degree of expertise as the preparer with regard to the proposed venture. As a result, numbers that intuitively make sense to the entrepreneur may still require explanation in the business plan. This literally may mean stating assumptions that relate line by line to the financial plan projections. Usually, however, this level of detail is unnecessary. Normally, stating certain key assumptions is sufficient to bring projections into proper focus.

The most important element in all of the projections, and the one that requires the greatest degree of support, is the anticipated sales volume. The credibility of this forecast is so important that an entire section in the marketing plan, rather than a single assumption, may be devoted to its support. As a consequence, the reviewer may well have received sufficient background regarding sales performance before he or she even turns to the financial plan. Still, it may be worthwhile to restate this support in summary form or add further insight. For the most part, the rest of the financial plan is an outgrowth of this critical element.

A second important assumption pertains to cost of goods sold and gross profit. This depends jointly on the cost of production or acquisition and pricing policy. Both the marketing section and operations section may shed light on this number. As a result, it is often sufficient to offer a simple explanation or percentage at this point in the plan.

Similarly, a complete set of assumptions should be developed for all of the projections contained in the financial plan. The entrepreneur must exercise careful judgment as to what degree of explanation is appropriate for each part of the financial plan. It is important to note that the nature of the business will dictate where such support is required.

For example, in an exotic, high technology business, the research and development budget may require careful explanation. In contrast, a more traditional company may not require any explanation of its modest research and development efforts.

In stating assumptions, it is useful to cite specific sources of information. As an illustration, a retail outlet might base sales and related inventory on an inventory turnover average provided by a specific trade association. Mention of the trade association helps legitimize the assumption. Depending on the complexity and extensiveness of assumptions, the entrepreneur should use discretion in deciding whether to combine all assumptions into a single statement, or provide a separate set of assumptions for each projection.

In making assumptions, one must bear in mind the inherent nature of projections. It is virtually impossible to eliminate all uncertainty. Rather, in the most brief and simple manner possible, the entrepreneur should try to elevate the confidence level of the reviewer regarding the company's ability to translate projections into operating reality.

Finally, it is important to note that entrepreneurs are often optimists. There is often too great a tendency on their part to assess a project's future in an overly positive light. For this reason, it has been suggested that several projections, based on different assumptions, be presented. In a similar vein, entrepreneurs should engage in "what if" analysis so that they fully understand the sensitivity of their business to certain critical factors.

For example, what happens to cash flow if, instead of extending 30 days' credit, a supplier will only ship raw materials C.O.D.? While all such scenarios need not be included in the business plan, this type of planning is invaluable in terms of allowing the entrepreneur a complete understanding of the financial nature of the business. In this age of personal computers and electronic spreadsheets, the generation of various financial scenarios is relatively easy.

NOTES AND ASSUMPTIONS FOR FINANCIAL PROJECTIONS

All financial statements have been projected on a quarterly basis and summarized annually.

Schedule 1: Projected Annual Income

Net Sales
For planning purposes, GFI has divided the national market into 15 equivalent regional markets. Rather than seek the outside investment necessary to mount a national campaign, the company plans to focus initially on two key markets, the Northeast and California. Equity investment, cash flows from these markets, and debt secured by inventory and accounts receivable will provide the funds necessary for further expansion.

The company expects to be operating in five of the 15 U.S. markets within five years, and sales projections assume entry into these markets in the following years.

Year	Number of markets
1	2
2	2
3	3
4	4
5	5

Sales for each market were projected using assumptions on the number of stores, the number of orders annually, and the average order size. Average order size and the average number of orders in the industry and target markets are provided by *Vick Products Sales Research Corporation.* Health-food-industry experts have advised the company that it can conservatively expect to gain a 75 percent distribution in the retail outlets of a given market area.

For each quarter and for each market the following formula was used:

Age Group	Average Order Size in $	Average Number of Orders	Average Number of Retail Outlets	Distribution	Total Sales Per Market
6-12 months	x	x	x	0.75	=
1-3 years	x	x	x	0.75	=

Total Sales per Market

A 50-percent distribution was assumed during the months immediately following entry into a new market. By the end of year one, 75-percent distribution is expected. Each market was expected to grow by 25 percent annually.

Based on information provided to GFI by *Vick Product Sales Research Corporation* and numerous industry experts, the company projects the following sales revenues and cost-of-sales percentages (see Attachments 14–3 and 14–4).

SALES REVENUES
($ thousands)

Year	Age 6–12 months	Age 1-3 years	Total Sales
1	$ 511	$ 705	$1,216
2	639	881	1,520
3	1,103	1,550	2,653
4	1,661	2,361	4,022
5	2,305	3,356	5,661

COST OF SALES (%)		
Year	Age 6-12 months	Age 1-3 years
1	51	49
2	51	49
3	50	50
4	50	50
5	50	50

First-year estimates are based on firm manufacturing price quotes that GFI has obtained verbally. The salaries of the premix operations staff have been included in cost of sales. The terms of all sales are assumed to be 45 days.

Payments to the manufacturer that will produce GFI products on a subcontractor basis comprise 85 percent of cost of sales. The remaining 15 percent represents raw material costs and direct labor for the purchase and preparation of premix that GFI will supply to the subcontractor (as mentioned in the section on manufacturing and operations). This group will also be responsible for quality control. The subcontractor will pay all other raw material costs and labor.

Operating Expenses

Research and development expenses include the salary of George Knapp—$60,000 annually—and, beginning in year three, an assistant at $25,000 annually.

Benefits for all GFI employees are estimated at 20 percent of their annual salaries. All salaries are assumed to increase at 10 percent per year.

Expenses of $125,000 related to the further testing of new products will be incurred and expensed in year one. These expenses for development and testing of new products are expected to increase at 10 percent per year.

Sales and marketing expenses based on the market plan outlined in the marketing section are:

Year One

Initial Marketing Campaign

Promotional products	$ 90,000
Test-market maintenance	18,000
Packaging design	55,000
Market planning	75,000
Market research, advertising and other promotional expenses	125,000
National sales manager (beginning second quarter year 1)	40,500
Miscellaneous	11,000
	$414,500

Year Two

Sales and marketing expenses are projected at 15 percent of sales. In the fourth quarter an additional $25,000 in promotional material and expenses and $18,000 in salary and benefits for the marketing director is included in preparation for entry into the third market.

Years Three through Five

Sales and marketing expenses are projected at 15 percent of sales plus $25,000 for promotional materials and expenses in the fourth quarter of each year in preparation for entry into additional market regions. Also, in the fourth quarter, an additional $7,500 in salary and benefits is included for the new sales assistants hired in the fourth quarter of years two and three.

General and administrative expenses are detailed in the following list. Administrative salaries include all employees not in the research, marketing, or premix production divisions.

Rent expense in years one and two is based on 3,500 square feet at $30 per square foot, with a 5-percent increase in the second year. In years three through five, rent expense is based on 5,000 square feet at $33 per square foot, with a 5-percent increase per year.

These rental costs include space that will be allocated to research, marketing, and sales activities. However, rental costs associated with premix preparation and quality testing have been treated as direct costs and included in the cost of sales estimates. The initial premix facility will be approximately 4,200 square feet (see facilities and properties).

GENERAL AND ADMINISTRATIVE EXPENSES
($ in thousands)

	Year 1	Year 2	Year 3	Year 4	Year 5
Salaries	$105	$181	$229	$256	$281
Benefits	21	36	46	51	56
Travel	21	28	35	43	54
Telephone	7	9	11	13	17
Utilities	5	10	10	13	15
Accounting and legal	40	40	50	55	60
Rent	105	110	132	139	146
Other	44	50	53	56	61
Total	$340	$464	$566	$626	$634

Amortization
Amortization to expense $163,000 in deferred start-up cost is projected on a straight-line basis over 10 years.

Interest Income
Cash balances at the beginning of the period are invested for that period at an average rate of 5 percent.

Interest Expense
Interest expense on short-term debt is charged at an 11.5-percent annual rate. Interest in year two is based on the $17,000 of short-term debt outstanding prior to equity financing that is repaid in the first quarter of the year.

A $50,000 loan was received before year one in the form of a one year note from a group of associates of the Drs. Knapp. An annual interest rate of 14 percent is carried on this loan.

Income Tax Expense
Income taxes are calculated at 50 percent of net income before taxes, less any tax-loss carryforwards, and are assumed to be paid in the

quarter in which they are incurred. Tax-loss carryforwards are estimated on a quarterly basis by adding retained earnings last quarter, if
negative, to the current quarter's net income.

Schedule 4: Projected Annual Cash Flow

A minimum cash balance of $15,000 per year is assumed for the pur-
poses of these projections.

Cash Receipts

Collections are assumed to be made in 45 days, based on discussions
with health food distributors. To simplify the projections, interest is
assumed to be received in the quarter in which it is earned. Equity
financing of $700,000 is assumed to be raised by issuance of addi-
tional shares of common stock.

Cash Disbursements

Projected direct labor relates entirely to production of the premix and
product quality testing, since production is carried out by a subcontractor. Raw material and manufacturing overhead include costs for
premix and payments to the subcontractor. Direct labor costs are assumed to be paid as incurred; all other expenses are assumed paid
within 30 days.

Capital expenditures in year one include $6,000 for office equip-
ment and $8,000 for a microcomputer and appropriate business soft-
ware. No other capital expenditures are anticipated in year one.

In the following years office equipment and other fixed asset additions are projected at 1 percent of sales. These items are included as
fixed assets on the balance sheet.

Long-term debt in this projection does not include repayment or additional borrowing. Long-term debt consists of a 10-year note with an
annual interest rate of 14 percent.

Interest expense is also assumed to be paid during the quarter in
which it is incurred.

Income tax expense is paid the quarter after it is incurred.

Short-Term Borrowing and Repayment

Short-term financing is assumed to be based on a revolving credit line with a maximum limit of 50 percent of the total accounts receivable and inventory balances in any quarter. Seventeen thousand dollars in short-term debt was borrowed to finance start-up activities. Repayment of this debt is included in the first quarter of year one. Additional funds are borrowed quarterly to cover cash shortfalls and maintain a minimum cash balance of $15,000. Short-term debt is repaid as funds become available.

Schedule 5: Projected Balance Sheet

Assets

Cash includes short-term investments. A minimum cash balance is assumed to be maintained through borrowing of short-term funds as necessary.

Accounts receivable are projected assuming a 45-day receivable period.

Inventory is projected based on an analysis of inventory turns in the health food industry and projected market expansion.

Fixed assets include the capital expenditures discussed previously. They are depreciated on a straight-line basis over five years.

Liabilities

Accounts payable include all trade payables and nonincometax accrued expenses. On average these expenses are paid in 30 days.

Short-term debt is projected to finance cash shortfalls in any quarter and to maintain a $15,000 minimum cash balance. Projected short-term debt is based on a revolving credit line that is repaid as funds become available. Interest on those funds is charged quarterly at an annual rate of 11.5 percent.

Taxes payable represents income tax expense for the fourth quarter in each year since income taxes are paid the quarter after they are incurred.

Long-term debt is entirely comprised of a $50,000 loan received prior to this proposed financing from a group of associates of the

Drs. Knapp. An annual interest rate of 14 percent is carried on this debt.

Owners Equity
Projected equity is comprised of initial equity of investment by the principals of $111,000 and $700,000 in additional equity financing projected in years one and two.

Retained earnings includes income and losses beginning in year one. All prior costs are included in deferred start-up costs and amortized over 10 years.

INCOME STATEMENTS

The purpose of an income statement is to capture in summary form the profit performance of a prospective venture. This projection is generally divided into revenues, cost of goods or services, expenses, and resulting pretax profit or loss. In many instances, it is appropriate to also show after-tax performance, since the tax effect of the venture is salient. The income statement is the most common—although not the most critical—indicator of financial performance for both start-up and existing ventures.

It is helpful to bear in mind the reviewer's objectives. A lender will be concerned primarily with a venture's viability. In most instances, at least interest, and often both interest and principal, are payable in the first month after a loan is made. Thus the capability to service debt usually must be demonstrated immediately. Profit potential is obviously attractive to a lender; however, because return is limited to a stated rate of interest, such potential is secondary to the ability to repay the loan.

In contrast, venture capitalists liberally share in a company's earnings, and thus have a primary interest in the company's growth potential. It is doubtful whether a venture capitalist would invest in a business simply because of the likelihood of viability.

The desires of a reviewer should influence the presentation of an income statement in terms of what elements are highlighted and the manner in which judgment is exercised in projecting returns.

1. Critical elements in the income statement should be scrutinized as they relate to sales volume, that is, as a percentage of sales. It is not at all unusual to present these percentages as a part of an income statement. They are often compared to industry benchmarks as a means of evaluating projected performance as well as credibility of the projection. Except in industries where such data are unavailable, such as new or quickly changing industries, the income statement should either be roughly consistent with industry averages or explanation should be offered where departures from these averages exist.

2. The numbers alone will mean little to the reviewer. An income statement can be prepared to show an enormous profit; yet, if such a profit is not a natural outgrowth of the rest of the business plan, it will mean little. The income statement, and in particular profit, should be consistent with the potential and limitations discussed in other sections. Inflated projections will detract from the plan's credibility.

3. This should reflect the business' tax status. A partnership or S corporation should include distributions to partners or stockholders once the business is operating profitably. Taxes should be estimated using an effective tax rate unless the business projects significant variations between income for accounting purposes and for tax purposes.

The following is the way GFI presented its income statement projections:

FIGURE 13–1. Schedule 1: Good Foods, Incorporated
Financial Projections (In thousands)[a]

| | Projected Annual Income ($ and % of Sales) | | | | | | | | | |
| | Year 1 | | Year 2 | | Year 3 | | Year 4 | | Year 5 | |
	Dollars	%	Dollars	%	Dollars	%	Dollars	%	Dollars	%
Net sales:										
Ages 6–12 months	511	42	639	42	1103	42	1661	41	2305	41
Ages 1–3 years	705	58	881	58	1550	58	2361	59	3356	59
Total sales	1216	100	1520	100	2653	100	4021	100	5661	100
Cost of sales:										
Ages 6–12 months	250	21	313	21	551	21	830	21	1152	20
Ages 1–3 years	360	30	441	29	775	29	1180	29	1678	30
Total cost of sales	610	50	754	50	1326	50	2011	50	2830	50
Gross margin	606	50	766	50	1327	50	2010	50	2831	50
Operating expenses:										
Research, dev., & eng.	197	16	217	14	268	10	295	7	325	6
Sales & marketing	415	34	366	24	430	16	636	16	849	15
Gen. & admin.	350	29	469	31	575	22	641	16	659	12
Total operating	962	79	1052	69	1274	48	1572	39	1833	32
Interest income	2	0	5	0	0	0	1	0	27	0
Interest expense	10	1	7	0	22	1	19	0	7	0
Net income (loss) before tax	(−364)	(−30)	(−288)	(−19)	31	1	420	10	1018	18
Tax expense	0	0	0	0	0	0	0	0	369	7
Net income after tax	−364	−30	−288	−19	31	1	420	10	649	11

[a]Note all figures have been rounded to nearest $1,000 or whole percentage.

154

SUMMARY OF HISTORICAL FINANCIAL DATA AND ESTIMATED BALANCE SHEET

Often, reviewers find it helpful to understand the history of the company in a financial format. The business plan can present a brief "history" of the sources and application of funds to show all receipts and expenditures from inception to date. This enables the reviewer to understand the financial history very quickly.

Similarly, the estimated balance sheet enables the reviewer to see the assets, liabilities and owners' equity at the time the plan was prepared. Other schedules or illustrations may give more detail later. However, these summaries enable the reviewer to have a quick reference point without detailed review of the financial projections.

FIGURE 13–2.   Schedule 2: Good Foods, Incorporated
Summary of Historical Financial Data

Sources of Funds:	
Equity Investments:	
Drs. George and Samuel Knapp	$ 58,500
Other investors	52,500
	$111,000
Loans:	
Loan proceeds	$ 67,000
Total sources	$178,000
Application of Funds:	
Deferred Start-Up Costs	
Research and development	$ 21,000
Marketing and promotion	1,900
Travel related to market research and product development	58,100
Legal and accounting	6,500
Office costs	22,400
Other operating costs	53,100
Total applications	$163,000
Net cash flow	$ 15,000

FIGURE 13–3.   Schedule 3: Good Foods,
Incorporated
Estimated Balance Sheet

Assets:	
Cash	**$ 15,000**
Deferred start-up costs	**163,000**
	$178,000
Liabilities and Owner's Equity	
Liabilities	
Short-term debt	**$ 17,000**
Long-term debt	**50,000**
	$ 67,000
Owners' Equity	
Equity	**$111,000**
	$178,000

GFI presented its Historical Financial Data and Estimated Balance Sheet as shown in Figures 13–2 and 13–3.

CASH FLOW STATEMENT

The most critical of all financial forecasts in a business plan is the cash flow projection. In many ways it is analogous to the income statement.

There are, however, some important distinctions. Instead of revenues and expenses, a cash flow statement reflects cash actually flowing into and out of the business. As a consequence, the bottom line of a cash flow statement reflects a company's net cash position, rather than its profit. A few adjustments can transform an income statement into a cash flow statement:

With respect to sales, an income statement reflects the earning of revenue. A cash flow reflects the actual receipt of cash from sales. In order to make this adjustment, one must be sensitive to anticipated payment terms for sales.

A cash flow statement reflects the receipt of all cash from all sources, including sales, the infusion of debt or equity proceeds, and the sale of or the liquidation of an asset. An income statement may not include all of these.

With respect to expenses, an income statement reflects expenses incurred, while a cash flow statement reflects the actual payment of these expenses. Some expenses may be paid immediately while others may be paid over a period of time. In order to make this adjustment, one must understand the nature of credit policies as they relate to a particular business.

An income statement reflects depreciation, because depreciation is an expense. However, since depreciation does not represent a cash obligation, it is not included in the cash flow statement. Conversely, repayment of loan principal is not considered an expense and therefore is not included in an income statement. It is, however, a cash obligation and is included in a cash flow statement.

Other cash requirements, such as acquisition of equipment or payment of dividends are not considered expenses. Therefore, they have an impact on cash flow, but not income.

It is important to understand that early in the company's lifetime, cash position will be more critical than profitability, because it more directly reflects the company's viability.

For example, a facility that provides medical care has an operating plan that anticipates significant profits in the first year of operation. However, assume that most bills are paid by third parties—insurance companies, Medicare, and Medicaid—and payment typically takes 90 to 120 days. While the facility might appear healthy on an annual profit and loss basis, there may be a critical cash bind in the initial months, when there are many cash obligations yet no cash inflow.

This start-up business will have plenty of "sales" volume, but no cash receipts. If such a facility did not begin with an adequate amount of working capital, it may be unable to meet its obligations, despite its profits. As a result, its survival might literally be threatened.

Other important points should be kept in mind when preparing a projected monthly cash flow:

1. The nature of most projections, financial and otherwise, is that they become more uncertain as one looks further into the future. Thus, while a quarterly or monthly cash flow is appropriate and even mandatory for the first 12 to 24 months, it is advisable to prepare quarterly cash flows in the mid-term and annual cash flows in the long term. These latter time intervals should correspond to the time intervals employed in the preparation of income statement projections.

2. A useful way to evaluate cash position at the end of a period is to translate the figure into periods of operating cash coverage. For example, if the ending cash position hovers at $50,000 and the monthly operating budget is $25,000, the company has 60 days' operating capital on hand. The appropriate level of operating capital will depend on a number of factors, including the speed with which receivables are collected, the consistency of cash flow, and the probability of critical problems and opportunities arising. In any event, the relationship between a desirable working capital level and the operating budget is important.

3. In formulating the capital requirement necessary to launch one's venture, it is almost impossible to determine the level of working capital needed without projecting monthly cash flow. This is the only method by which one may predict when cash shortfalls will occur, and the extent of these shortfalls.

4. As is the case with an income statement, a monthly cash flow, if prepared carefully, can represent the basis for an operating budget and a set of objectives against which one can manage and evaluate actual performance.

BALANCE SHEET AND FINANCIAL RATIOS AND STATISTICS

Rather than reflecting performance over a period of time, a balance sheet allows a "snapshot" of a company's financial strengths and weaknesses at a particular point in time. A balance sheet summarizes the company's assets (what it owns), liabilities (what it owes), and net worth (the difference between assets and liabilities). Assets are typically classified as

FIGURE 13–4.   Schedule 4: Good Foods, Incorporated
Projected Annual Cash Flow[a]

	Year 1	Year 2	Year 3	Year 4	Year 5
Beginning cash balance	15	15	15	15	99
Cash receipts:					
Collections	1022	1524	2497	3840	5458
Interest	2	5	1	1	27
Long-term debt	0	0	0	0	0
Equity financing	450	250	0	0	0
Total receipts	1474	1779	2498	3842	5486
Disbursements:					
Operating expenses	879	1025	1252	1531	1795
Dir. labor costs	31	39	68	103	142
Raw materials	474	660	1112	1693	2358
Mfg. overhead less dep.	56	78	131	199	277
Capital expenditures	21	15	27	40	57
Long-term debt	0	0	0	0	0
Interest expense	10	7	22	19	7
Income tax expense	0	0	0	0	234
Total disbursements	1471	1825	2612	3585	4869
Net cash flow	3	−45	−114	257	616
Cash before loans	18	−30	−99	272	715
Short-term borrowing	64	59	114	0	0
Short-term repayments	67	14	0	173	0
Ending cash balance	15	15	15	99	715

[a] Note all figures have been rounded to nearest $1,000 or whole percentage.

"current," such as cash, inventory, and accounts receivable; "fixed," such as plant and equipment; and "intangible," such as good will and licenses. Liabilities are normally categorized as being "current" (due within one year) or "long-term" (due after one year).

When reviewed alone, any single element on a balance sheet will have little meaning. However, when all elements are examined relative to one another, a great deal can be inferred about the company's financial health. Even more can be learned when one views the balance sheet in conjunction with the company's income statement.

Some of the measures typically calculated in order to assess projected or historical performance are:

Liquidity Ratios. These ratios, such as the current and quick ratios, typically compare all or some of the company's current assets to its current liabilities. They suggest how capable the company is to meet its debt obligations in the near term.

Asset Management Ratios. These ratios, such as inventory turnover and accounts receivable turnover, give one a sense of how efficiently and effectively a company is employing the assets at its disposal.

Debt Ratios. These ratios, such as debt-to-equity, help place in perspective how the company is capitalized and, more precisely, how highly the company is leveraged. These ratios can help one understand the company's stability and its capacity to raise further capital.

As in the case of income statements, industries are often marked by certain financial characteristics. Companies in one industry may be highly leveraged. Those in another might enjoy a rapid turnover of inventory. Since the reviewer will rely on such benchmarks to evaluate the start-up, deviations from industry averages should be explained.

The company's opening balance sheet—the balance sheet that is anticipated at the start of the business—is relatively simple to prepare in that it reflects the amount of capital to be raised for the start-up. Specifically, it presents how the capital is to be spent (the assets that will be acquired) and how this capital will be raised (sources of debt and equity).

Balance sheets should also be projected for the end of the company's first three to five years. These balance sheets will be a direct outgrowth of the opening balance sheet and intervening events such as the company's financial performance, changes in operating characteristics such as faster collection of accounts receivable, and subsequent infusions of equity and debt capital.

The following points are worth considering when preparing projected balance sheets:

1. First-time entrepreneurs sometimes mistakenly believe that it is possible to fund a company's start-up entirely through debt. This is analogous to attempting to buy a house with no down payment. In almost all instances, lenders require that some portion of the capitalization be provided through equity.

2. Most sophisticated lenders and investors want to see that a significant financial commitment has been made by the entrepreneur. Usually this means a commitment that is significant in light of the entrepreneur's personal financial resources. The rationale behind this is that after such a commitment has been made, the entrepreneur is locked into the venture. Should the venture encounter rocky times, the entrepreneur will not be able to walk away without incurring personal financial loss and will therefore devote full and best efforts to the success of the enterprise.

3. Liquidity is critical in the case of a young or infant company whose future is uncertain. Adequate liquidity will permit the company to weather unexpected difficulties and exploit unanticipated opportunities.

4. It is not unusual for a start-up operation to experience losses in its initial stages. Thus funding needed subsequent to the start-up often cannot be generated internally. Rather, later

rounds of financing which are sometimes critical for growth frequently must be sought from external sources—either lenders or investors.

The entrepreneur should recognize this, attempt to anticipate subsequent capital requirements accurately, and plan for these infusions in advance. Perhaps the worst time to seek capital is when the company desperately requires it.

A situation viewed as a crisis by the entrepreneur will probably not be pressing to the investor or lender unless he or she already has funds at risk in the venture. The funding source will desire adequate time to review the request. If pressured, the response will probably be negative. Even if the response is positive, a frantic request clearly weakens the entrepreneur's bargaining position and likely will result in the capital infusion being more costly.

In addition, some business plans include certain statistics and financial ratios they believe might be important to the reviewer. These ratios and statistics should include a method of calculation and some discussion of why they are meaningful to the company.

GFI presented its balance sheet projections as financial ratios as follows:

FIGURE 13–5.   Schedule 5: Good Foods, Incorporated
Projected Annual Balance Sheets[a]

	Opening Balance	Year 1	Year 2	Year 3	Year 4	Year 5
Assets:						
Cash	15	15	15	15	99	715
Accounts receivable	0	194	190	346	527	730
Inventory	0	12	37	72	113	118
Fixed assets	0	21	36	63	103	160
Accum. depreciation	0	−2	−7	−16	−32	−57
Deferred start-up costs	163	147	130	114	98	82
Total assets	178	387	402	593	908	1747

FIGURE 13–5.   *(Continued)*

Liabilities:						
Accounts payable	0	141	166	228	311	382
Short-term debt	17	14	59	173	0	0
Taxes payable	0	0	0	0	0	135
Long-term debt	50	50	50	50	50	50
Total liabilities	**67**	**205**	**274**	**451**	**361**	**567**
Owners equity:						
Capital stock	111	561	811	811	811	811
Retained earnings	0	-380	-684	-668	-264	369
Total equity	**111**	**181**	**127**	**143**	**547**	**1180**
Total liabilities & equity	**178**	**387**	**402**	**593**	**908**	**1747**

[a] Note all figures have been rounded to nearest $1,000 or whole percentage.

Good Foods, Incorporated
Projected Annual Financial Ratios

	Year 1	Year 2	Year 3	Year 4	Year 5
Inventory turns	68	36	25	22	24
Days receivables	46	46	46	46	46
Days payables	30	30	30	30	30
Gross profit/sales	49.8%	50.4%	50.0%	50.0%	50.0%
Net income/sales	0.0%	0.0%	0.6%	10.1%	11.2%
Debt/equity	35.1%	85.4%	156.1%	9.1%	4.2%
Return on equity	0.0%	0.0%	10.8%	73.9%	53.6%
Return on assets	0.0%	0.0%	2.6%	44.5%	36.2%
Return on investment	0.0%	0.0%	1.9%	49.8%	78.0%
Current ratio	1.42	1.08	1.08	2.38	3.02

BREAK-EVEN ANALYSIS

Although GFI did not, it is sometimes helpful to include in the financial section a break-even analysis, which demonstrates that level of sales that must be attained in order for a company to meet cash obligations, such as operating expenses and debt repayment, internally. Such analysis is mechanical and the necessary assumptions sometimes reduce its precision.

Regardless, it does afford a rough estimate of the volume that must be generated for the company to break even. This type of analysis is usually more meaningful to a lender than an investor, since lenders are primarily concerned with viability and capacity to service debt while an investor typically seeks a significant rate of return. In either case, a break-even analysis does help to define a major milestone in the company's life, the point at which cash generated from sales is sufficient to address all cash obligations.

The step-by-step procedure for calculating break-even is:

1. Segregate all cash obligations into fixed or variable obligations. A fixed obligation is one that does not vary with the level of sales, such as debt repayment. A variable obligation is one that does vary as a function of sales, such as cost of goods sold.

   It should be noted that many obligations will not be purely fixed or variable. For instance, total payroll might include office payroll, which is fixed, and production payroll, which is variable. In such an instance, one should do one's best to separate such an obligation into fixed and variable components.

2. A total fixed and a total variable cost figure should be calculated. Total fixed obligations will be stated as an absolute number, such as $100,000. Total variable cost will be stated as a percentage of sales, such as 60 percent.

3. These figures should then be inserted into the following formula.

$$\text{Break-even Sales} = \frac{\text{Fixed costs}}{\text{Contribution margin}}$$

Where Contribution Margin = 1 − variable costs as a percentage of sales

Therefore:

$$\text{Break-even Sales} = \frac{\$100,000}{1 - .60}$$

$$\text{Break-even Sales} = \$250,000$$

These calculations suffer from a number of limitations. Perhaps most importantly, there are typically different break-even levels of sales depending on the size of operation. Viewed in the proper light, however, this calculation will afford the reviewer a general idea as to what volume is required in order for a company to become self-supporting. This analysis is particularly enlightening when viewed in comparison to a projected income statement.

PRODUCT AND SERVICE SPECIFIC FINANCIAL SUMMARIES

It is often worthwhile to explain the importance of each product or service relative to the company's total scope of activity. Typically, this involves identifying the contribution margin of a specific product or service, or some group of products and services.

Mechanically, this can be accomplished by segregating sales figures and then, where possible, assigning expenses associated with each sales-generating activity. There will be some expenses that cannot readily be allocated in this manner. Some examples of this might include administrative payroll or interest expense. There is no reason or rationale for allocating such overhead to a specific product or activity. Rather, the difference between sales and associated expenses represents the contribution to overhead and profit for that product or activity. This in itself is meaningful in assessing the relative importance of each of the business's products or services.

Alternatively, it may be sufficient to communicate such information visually, using charts reflecting gross sales, gross profit, and operating profit. The mode of representation or whether to present such data is up to the entrepreneur. To decide, one must ask whether such information facilitates a significantly better understanding of the business.

COMMENT: FINANCIAL PLAN

GFI is both detailed and professional in its presentation of anticipated financial performance. Most important, the plan offers a comprehensive set of assumptions. Without these, evaluating performance would be a far more difficult task.

Performance is presented five years into the future on an annual basis. While this is fine for a "first cut" presentation in a business plan, one would hope GFI has projected performance on a quarterly or even monthly basis as well, at least for the first two years.

For both planning and reviewing purposes, the greater detail is meaningful, particularly in the early years before positive cash flow has been established.

The company shows us only one set of projections, which we can assume is a "most likely," scenario. With the aid of electronic spreadsheets, it would not be difficult for GFI to play some "what if" games and prepare both optimistic and pessimistic scenarios.

It should be noted that GFI saves some product-line profitability statements and sales analysis for the appendix. This is fine, so long as they are clearly presented and easily found.

14

ATTACHMENTS TO THE BUSINESS PLAN

What to include as attachments to a business plan is highly dependent on the type of business, the kinds of products or services it will offer, and the complexity of the plan itself.

Attachments should not be used just to "wow" a reviewer, but should add to the reviewer's understanding should he or she desire to know more than what is presented in the body of the plan, and to add credibility to statements made in the plan, especially if they are complex and time-consuming to explain.

Some plans arrive at reviewers' offices with no supporting documentation, others with boxes of such attachments. In most cases, it is best not to burden the reviewer, and if you have a number of support documents, you may want to create an index and one-page summaries of each, letting the reviewer know that the full document will be sent on request.

The attachments that follow, from the GFI plan, are illustrative of some of the more common attachments sent with business plans.

ATTACHMENT 14–1
MANAGEMENT RESUMES

Judith M. Appel

RELEVANT EXPERIENCE	RESPONSIBLE FOR
Owner/President Nature's Best, Inc. Good Foods, Inc. 1985–present	Managing all aspects of the business operations
Marketing Director Healthy Harvest Foods, Inc. Yonkers, NY 1982–1985	Managing the marketing, personnel and budgets for all product lines
Director of Volunteers and Public Relations Children's Hospital for Special Services White Plains, NY 1980–1982	Determining scheduling of personnel and representing hospital in community
Nutritionist Hospital for Children Brooklyn Heights, NY 1977–1980	Planning all meals for Heights patients and staff
Pediatric Assistant and and Technician Pediatric Clinic Baltimore, MD 1974–1977	Assisting pediatrician in patient care

ORGANIZATION AND MEMBERSHIP

Consultant
Cancer Forum, 1988–present
National Association of Child Care Management, 1980–present
National Health Federation, 1987
The Hunger Project, 1982–1985

Board Member
Child Welfare League of America, 1983–1987
National Health Institute, 1980–1984

HEALTH RELATED EDUCATION

Nutritional Needs of Newborn Children
International Childcare Institute
April 1987

Transitional Nutrition for Children
National Nutrition Center
June, July 1986

The International Cancer Symposium
Omega Institute
1985

ACADEMIC EDUCATION

Pace University
Graduate School of Business
New York, NY
MBA, Marketing
1982

Johns Hopkins University Night School
Baltimore, MD
MS, Nutrition
1977

University of Maryland
College Park, MD
BS, Biology
1974

Dr. George P. Knapp

RELEVANT EXPERIENCE	RESPONSIBLE FOR
Vice President, Research and Development Good Foods, Inc. 1988–present	Developing an advanced line of complete health food meals
Nutrition Consultant Heights Hospital for Children Brooklyn Heights, NY 1988–present	Contributing to the Heights planning of balanced meals for pediatric patients
Acting Director Heights Hospital for Children Brooklyn Heights, NY 1987–1988	Coordination of the operations of the hospital
Director, Department of Pediatrics Children's Hospital for Special Services White Plains, NY 1978–1984	Managing pediatric functions and acting in medical capacity
Consultant in Pediatric Oncology Treatment Cancer Therapy Unit Henry Bergh Memorial Hospital New York, NY 1976–1978	Consulting on cancer patient diagnoses
Associate Physician Brooklyn Children's Hospital Brooklyn, NY 1973–1976	Patient care

CURRENTLY

Consultant   Nature's Best, Inc.
                  Directing the development of a complete,
                  nontoxic line of health foods for children

Member   Board of Directors for Heights Hospital for
                  Children
                  Children's Health and Nutrition Council
                  Pennsauken, NJ
                  American Pediatric Holistic Medical Association
                  Belair, MD

EDUCATION

University of Pennsylvania
School of Medicine
Doctor of Medicine (MD), 1972

George Washington University
Washington, DC
Bachelor of Science Biology, 1968

International Cancer Symposium, 1981
Omega Institute

LECTURES

Children's Nutrition lectures at:
  Pittsburgh Children's Hospital
  National Institute of Health
  Gerber Baby Foods

NUTRITION PAPERS PRESENTED

Holistic Pediatric Medicine
National Child Nutrition Center
Rochester, NY
April 1984

Lincoln College Preparatory School
Philadelphia, PA

ARTICLES AND RADIO BROADCASTS

PAPERS PUBLISHED

"A Natural Approach to Child Nutrition," *Redbook's Young Mother*, October 1988

"Children's Common Health Problems," *Whole Life Times*, September 1987

RADIO PROGRAMS

Holistic Parenting
WNYC
September 1988

Cappy's World
WVIP
Children and Prevention of Disease
August 1986

Dr. Samuel Knapp

RELEVANT EXPERIENCE	RESPONSIBLE FOR
Consultant Nature's Best, Inc. Good Foods, Inc. Present	Developing the health food line
Owner/Partner, Physician Heights Hospital for Children Brooklyn Heights, NY Present	Patient care and consultation
Staff Instructor Child Welfare League of America New York, NY 1981–1988	Conducting seminars on child nutrition
Associate Physician Heights Hospital for Children Brooklyn Heights, NY 1981	Patient care
Associate Physician Dr. Phillip Weber Hoboken, NJ 1979	Patient care

EDUCATION

Cornell University College of Medicine
New York, NY
Doctor of Medicine (MD), 1979

George Washington University
Bachelor of Science, 1975

International Cancer Symposium, 1987
Omega Institute

PUBLICATIONS

"The Holistic Approach to Treating Your Child," *The Health Quarterly Plus Two,* November/December 1991

"The Child Nutrition Controversy," *The Health Quarterly Plus Two,* January/February 1990

"Holistic Pediatric Medicine," *Parent's Magazine,* December 1987

"A Holistic Approach to Child Nutrition," Child Welfare League of America Monograph No. 137, January 1987

"An Overview of Disease," *American Family,* Spring 1986

Major contributor to a book on holistic pediatric medicine, involving 50 pediatricians internationally, *Growth and Disease: A Holistic Approach,* edited by Robert Lombardi and published by Bobbs-Merrill in 1990.

LECTURES

Caring for Your Child
Leisure Classes, Inc.
White Plains, NY
February/March 1990

RADIO PROGRAMS

Cappy's World
WVIP
Children and Prevention of Disease
August 1989

Holistic Parenting
WNYC
January 1988

Children's Nutrition
WNYC
November 1988

ATTACHMENT 14–2
COMPETITIVE ANALYSIS

FIGURE 14–1. Competitive Analysis.

Company	Product Benefits	Advertising/Promotion	Sales/Distribution	Products
Health Valley	No additives, preservatives No chemicals, insecticides, etc. Palatability	Advertises in HF magazines Good display of products Good packaging Good handout information	Ships direct Some HF distributors	Cereal
Familia	No additives, preservatives No chemicals, insecticides, etc. Industry leader	National health journals and radio Provides nutritional hotline Good packaging Booth at trade shows	Uses own sales force Uses HF distributors	Cereal
Gerber	No salt or preservatives Different foods for different stages of development	Advertises in national magazines	Uses own sales force Uses supermarket distributors	Variety of meats, vegetables, fruits, desserts, juices, cereals
Beech-Nut	No salt or preservatives Different foods for different stages of development	Advertises in national magazines	Uses own sales force Uses supermarket distributors	Variety of meats, vegetables, fruits, desserts, juices, cereals
Heinz	No salt or preservatives Different foods for different stages of development	Advertises in national magazines	Uses own sales force Uses supermarket distributors	Variety of meats, vegetables, fruits, desserts, juices, cereals

ATTACHMENT 14–3
PROJECTION OF SALES BY
MARKET LINE

FIGURE 14–2.   Ages 6–12 months (sales by market).

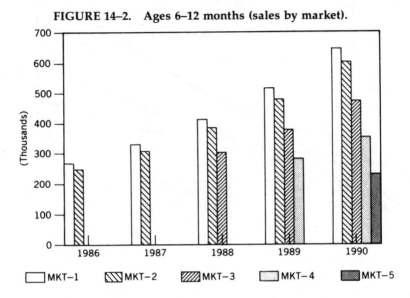

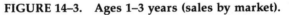

FIGURE 14–3.   Ages 1–3 years (sales by market).

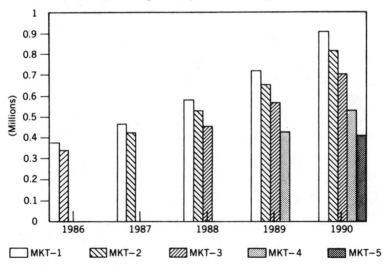

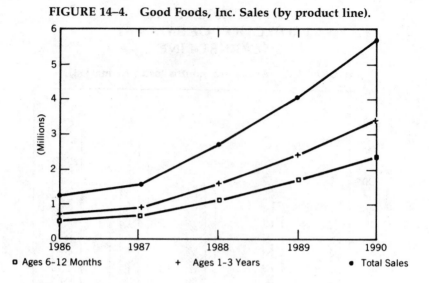

FIGURE 14–4. Good Foods, Inc. Sales (by product line).

ATTACHMENT 14–4
PRODUCT
LINE PROFIT ANALYSIS

FIGURE 14-5.   Product Line Profit Analysis.

Ages 6–12 Months

Product	Number of Cases Ordered	Quantity Per Case	Price Per Case	Revenue Per Order	Cost Per Order		Profit Per Order	
					%	%	%	%
Dinners	5	36/ 4.5 oz.	$14.40	$ 72.00	$ 38.90	54	$ 33.10	46
Meats	6	36/ 4.5 oz.	$10.80	$ 64.80	$ 33.00	51	$ 31.80	49
Vegetables	6	36/ 4.5 oz.	$10.80	$ 64.80	$ 32.40	50	$ 32.40	50
Desserts	5	36/ 4.5 oz.	$10.80	$ 54.00	$ 27.00	50	$ 27.00	50
Fruits	6	36/ 4.5 oz.	$10.80	$ 64.80	$ 33.00	51	$ 31.80	49
Biscuits, cookies	4	12/10 oz.	$13.20	$ 52.80	$ 28.00	53	$ 24.80	47
				$373.20	$192.30	51	$180.90	49

Ages 1–3 Years

Product	Number of Cases Ordered	Quantity Per Case	Price Per Case	Revenue Per Order	Cost Per Order		Profit Per Order	
					$	%	%	%
Dinners	4	36/ 4.5 oz.	$14.40	$ 57.60	$ 31.10	54	$ 26.50	46
Meats	4	36/ 4.5 oz.	$10.80	$ 43.20	$ 22.00	51	$ 21.20	49
Vegetables	4	36/ 4.5 oz.	$10.80	$ 43.20	$ 21.60	50	$ 21.60	50
Desserts	6	36/ 4.5 oz.	$10.80	$ 64.80	$ 32.40	50	$ 32.40	50
Fruits	3.5	36/ 4.5 oz.	$10.80	$ 37.80	$ 19.30	51	$ 18.50	49
Biscuits, cookies	3	12/10 oz.	$13.20	$ 39.60	$ 21.00	53	$ 18.60	47
Prepared foods	4	42/ 6 oz.	$37.80	$151.20	$ 81.60	54	$ 69.60	46
Sandwich meats	6	24/12 oz.	$14.40	$ 86.40	$ 44.90	52	$ 41.50	48
				$523.80	$273.90	49	$249.90	51

FIGURE 14–6. Product Line Profit Analysis.

Ages 6–12 Months

Product	Number of Cases Ordered	Quantity Per Case	Price Per Case	Revenue Per Order	Cost Per Order $	%	Profit Per Order $	%
Dinners	4	36/ 4.5 oz.	$14.40	$ 57.60	$ 31.10	54	$ 26.50	46
Meats	6	36/ 4.5 oz.	$10.80	$ 64.80	$ 33.00	51	$ 31.80	49
Vegetables	5.4	36/ 4.5 oz.	$10.80	$ 58.30	$ 29.20	50	$ 29.10	50
Desserts	5	36/ 4.5 oz.	$10.80	$ 54.00	$ 27.00	50	$ 27.00	50
Fruits	6	36/ 4.5 oz.	$10.80	$ 64.80	$ 33.00	51	$ 31.80	49
Biscuits, cookies	4	12/10 oz.	$13.20	$ 52.80	$ 28.00	53	$ 24.80	47
				$352.30	$181.30	51	$171.00	49

Ages 1–3 Years

Product	Number of Cases Ordered	Quantity Per Case	Price Per Case	Revenue Per Order	Cost Per Order $	%	Profit Per Order $	%
Dinners	3	36/ 4.5 oz.	$14.40	$ 43.20	$ 23.30	54	$ 19.90	46
Meats	3	36/ 4.5 oz.	$10.80	$ 32.40	$ 16.50	51	$ 15.90	49
Vegetables	3	36/ 4.5 oz.	$10.80	$ 32.40	$ 16.20	50	$ 16.20	50
Desserts	5	36/ 4.5 oz.	$10.80	$ 54.00	$ 27.00	50	$ 27.00	50
Fruits	2	36/ 4.5 oz.	$10.80	$ 21.60	$ 11.00	51	$ 10.60	49
Biscuits, cookies	4	12/10 oz.	$13.20	$ 52.80	$ 28.00	53	$ 24.80	47
Prepared foods	4	42/ 6 oz.	$37.80	$151.20	$ 81.60	54	$ 69.60	46
Sandwich meats	6	24/12 oz.	$14.40	$ 86.40	$ 44.90	52	$ 41.50	48
				$474.00	$248.50	49	$225.50	51

ATTACHMENT 14–5
SAMPLE AGREEMENT OF CONFIDENTIALITY

This letter will serve to confirm our agreement and understanding concerning the confidential nature of certain information, business plans, ideas, processes, designs, products, technical specifications, discoveries, data, trade secrets, and other proprietary information (collectively the "Information"), disclosed by _____ which may have been, or may in the future be disclosed to _____.

In return for disclosing the information to _____ has agreed to retain such information in confidence and not to publish, make available or otherwise disclose any part or portion of such information to any third party except with the prior express written consent of an authorized representative of _____, unless such information can be shown by documentary evidence to be in the public domain. Such information shall not be considered to be in the public domain merely because it is suggested by more general information or could be assembled from one or more sources or has become available to the public by virtue of a breach of this Agreement or a similar agreement by another person or entity. In addition, _____ has agreed to use its best efforts and all reasonable precautions to assure that such information disclosed to _____ verbally, by written material, by electronic data storage media, or by any other means is properly protected from unauthorized disclosure to any third party.

_____ has also agreed not to make any copies of any materials that may be given to _____ and to return all copies of such material immediately upon the request of _____. _____ further agrees that all such information is owned by _____ and is confidential, valuable and essential to the ongoing conduct of _____'s business. _____ has further agreed not to use, exploit, and/or commercialize such information for _____ benefit or the benefit of other third parties.

This Agreement shall not be construed as granting any license or other rights to _____.

We agree to be legally bound by the terms of this Agreement of Confidentiality and have executed it this _____ day of _____ 1993.

By: _____   By: _____
                               For

15

FURTHER CONSIDERATIONS

While a business plan modeled on this book's format will be sufficiently detailed for a reviewer, there are a number of further considerations one needs to begin thinking through during the business-plan writing phase. Some of these considerations may be explicitly stated in the business plan, but most will not.

However, it might be useful to consider these issues for planning and scenario-building purposes as you build the business plan.

These considerations fall into two main categories: people and money. All good business ideas grow into successful businesses on these two vines. And like vines, people and money are constantly entangled with one another.

PEOPLE

A business needs to attract and retain the best employees possible, all the way from the executive suite to the shop floor. In order to do this, a business must develop a compensation plan and a set of incentives that motivate people and develop employee commitment.

Developing such a plan early can serve to eliminate the threat of key people leaving down the road. Everything from a comprehensive benefit plan to stock ownership or stock options should be considered. Key questions include what benefits, incentives and types of compensation will be available to all employees, what of these will be reserved for executives (using an advisor well versed in tax and other regulations regarding limitations to compensation) and what special incentives might be offered to key people.

While many large companies have employee-benefit packages that typically include health insurance, group life and/or disability, vacation and sick time, and a qualified retirement or profit-sharing plan, small entrepreneurial companies can often not afford these benefits.

Stock can either be given to employees—usually to executives in lieu of cash—or an option can be given to buy stock at a set price.

Some people argue not to give employees too much in a new company because they will keep coming back for more and the precedent will have been set for future employees. Others argue that in a world where talented and dedicated workers are perceived as being integral to long-term success, a company must "do the right thing" from the start to attract and retain dedicated employees. You have to answer the questions: "Can I afford the best? Can I afford not to have the best?"

At the same time you are wrestling with how to attract, motivate, and retain the best by incentive, you also need to determine whether you want to hold onto those you attract by way of personal agreements. This issue is especially important in the management arena. Two common tools for retaining executive talent are the employment agreement, which sets a specific time during which an executive and a company agree to team up, and a non-compete agreement, which sets a time after an executive leaves during which he or she may not go to work for a competitor, or in the industry, or in the region.

Many times these two agreements are tied together. For instance, Mr. A. comes to work for you with a three-year contract to be Chief Executive Officer, and a noncompete agreement that goes for two years after that. Ms. B., who's company you have bought out, is given a seven-year "consulting"/non-compete contract (she will really actively work for about an 18-month transition period, then be paid simply in exchange for not competing).

MONEY

While issues involving people may be more emotionally complex, issues involving money are often more dynamic and fluid. A strategy you employ when first looking for capital will have ramifications for your position and financial stake in the company—and your ultimate success. This is especially true when looking for equity financing.

The question boils down to: "Should I raise money early, giving up a larger share for the security of not having to go into the capital market too late or repeatedly; or do I give up less now and risk having to go back into the market when conditions make it more difficult?"

Put another way, the question is: "Should I sell cheaper stock now and have to give more of it to raise the capital I need, or give away less later when the stock is more expensive?"

Then there is the question of how much a company really needs. Entrepreneurs are notorious for underestimating their capital needs. One very successful company started out a decade ago looking for $500,000. An advisor suggested that the entrepreneur ask for $1 million on the theory "take what you think you need and double it." A funding source loved the concept and employed the same theory again, offering $2 million. Two million barely got the company over the initial financial hump and on its way.

If the company had taken $500,000 and used it, there may not have been another investor for a second round. The company, which today generates several hundred million dollars in revenue annually, may have failed had it been undercapitalized.

CASHING OUT

The place where people and money come together in the most forceful way is around the question of cashing out. Whether an individual or institution has lent money, invested in equity, or invested time and effort, the question is always: "What does the pot at the end of the rainbow look like?"

If you're an entrepreneur, you're a combination of visionary and chief-cook-and-bottle-washer. You're worrying about next week, or next month, or the next stage of growth and development. But, just like a chess grandmaster, you also need to begin plotting the end game right from the first move.

Venture capitalists have to see the exit door and understand how long it will take to get there before becoming interested. This is especially true for those venture funds which are obligated to liquidate and redistribute their holdings within a limited period.

Lenders don't necessarily need to see the exit door for the relationship, but they need to see the end of the current obligation. Lenders are more comfortable with what they know, and they would rather lend money to a business in an industry with a well-established exit route—say dry cleaning or small commercial printing/photocopying centers—than with one that is speculative or has no good way to assess marketplace value.

People who come into the organization, especially those who receive noncash compensation, hope that they are signing their employment agreements and noncompetes in exchange for stock, options, warrants, and the like that will be worth something when they leave, either on an open market or by selling it back to the company.

The more these issues are explored, at least in early drafts of the business plan, the more valuable the plan will be to you as a planning and decision-support document. And the more these issues are explored, the easier it will be for you to evaluate competing offers from funding sources.

When dealing with all three of these issues—people, money, and the cash out—remember that timing is everything; what's right today may not be right tomorrow. You need to anticipate events as well as possible. Remember also, these are exactly the kind of issues with which professional advisors and even boards of directors can be very helpful, both as a sounding board and because of their experience with these issues in other businesses or with other clients.

CONCLUSION

If there is one message we hope to leave you with, it is that good ideas make good businesses, and good businesses make good business plans. The best business plan can't turn a bad idea into a good business.

A good business plan, however, can help to make a good business credible, understandable, and attractive to someone who is unfamiliar with the business. Writing a good business plan—and more importantly, thinking through a good business plan before writing it, can't guarantee success, but it can go a long way toward reducing the odds of failure.

We hope this guide has been helpful.

INDEX

Numbers in **boldface** refer to entries that only appear in the Good Foods Incorporated (GFI) Business Plan Model.